KitchenAid®

Convection Oven Cook Book

By the Editors of Sunset Books and Sunset Magazine

Sunset Publishing Corporation • Menlo Park, California

Supervising Editor: **Elizabeth Hogan**

Research and Text: **Cynthia Scheer**

Staff Editor: **Anne K. Turley**
Photography: **Nikolay Zurek**
Photo Editor: **Lynne B. Morrall**
Design: **Joe di Chiarro**
Illustrations: **Susan Jaekel**

Cover: Show off one of convection cooking's strong points—roasting—with Herb Cheese Cornish Hens (recipe on page 35), crisply browned on the outside, succulent and juicy on the inside. Offer with slices of crusty French bread to mop up the melted cheese inside the hens. Other accompaniments include bright cherry tomatoes and dry white wine. Photographed by Nikolay Zurek.

Editor, Sunset Books: Elizabeth L. Hogan

Special Printing for KitchenAid
April 1992

CONTENTS

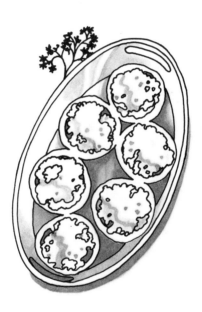

Cooking with Hot Air

Roasted meats perfectly browned on all sides, even-textured breads with golden crusts, soufflés puffed higher than you thought possible—these are a few of convection cooking's palate-pleasing advantages. Its energy-saving advantages include cutting cooking time as much as 30 percent and reducing oven temperatures.

What's more, convection cooking also turns out tender baked fish; juicy, crisp-skinned poultry; and delicious pastries and desserts of all types. In fact, any dish you'd ordinarily bake in a standard gas or electric oven can be cooked satisfactorily in a convection oven, but roasted and baked items are its strong points.

Convection oven advantages

- You don't have to baste meats or poultry; juices are sealed in.
- Delicate foods don't get overly dry.
- For most kinds of roasting and baking, you don't have to preheat the oven.
- You can fill the oven racks to capacity without affecting cooking time—just leave a little airspace between pans, and between pans and oven sides.
- No special bakeware is required.
- Convection ovens can be used to dry fruits and vegetables.
- You can set bread to rise in the oven.

- Puff pastry, soufflés, and foods with leavening agents (yeast, beaten egg whites, baking powder) rise higher because temperature is constant.

Professional chefs know all about convection cooking; convection ovens have been used in restaurants for years. Now the convection-cooking principle of fan-circulated hot air has been adapted for home use.

In your KitchenAid convection oven, heated air is driven by a fan under and around foods for fast, even cooking and browning. The convection method speeds baking, roasting, and broiling. Moreover, your oven is suitable for multi-level baking, thanks to a circular heating element surrounding the fan; the fan distributes the heat from the rear, allowing for even browning of large quantities of food being baked at the same time.

For this book we've selected a wide range of dishes—some quick and easy recipes for family fare, some more complicated dishes for special occasions. We've also included a variety of cooking methods. For instance, in the "Meats" chapter you'll find recipes for juicy, tender roasts seasoned to perfection, as well as for casseroles, stews, and slow-cooked meats.

Actually, the recipes throughout the book are intended to help you use your convection oven to its full potential. That's the raison d'être for this cook book—to show you how to have the courage of your convections and use the hot air method of cooking to its best advantage.

(Continued on next page)

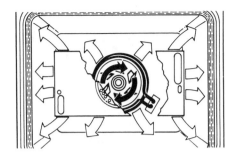

Convection bake

The rear element operates at full power whenever heating. Air in the oven cavity is circulated by the fan for even heating. Use this setting for foods requiring gentle cooking, such as pastries and soufflés, and for baking yeast breads, quick breads, and cakes. This setting is also recommended when baking large quantities of baked goods at one time.

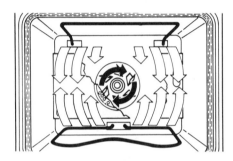

Convection roast

The bottom element and outer top element operate at full power and glow red whenever heating. Air in the oven cavity is circulated by the fan for even heating and faster cooking. Use this setting for baking and roasting.

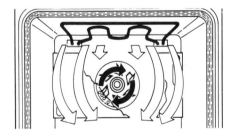

Convection broil

The top element operates at full power whenever heating. Air in the oven cavity is circulated by the fan for even heating with the same results as a rotisserie. Use this setting for broiling thick cuts of meat.

WHAT IS HOT-AIR COOKING?

The word "convection" means "the act of conveying." In this case, heat is conveyed by moving air. Every convection oven has a small fan to circulate the hot air. Some manufacturers put the fan on top, others put it on the side or in the back. The effect is virtually the same, regardless of the design: the fan circulates air past the source of heat (usually an electric element, sometimes a gas flame) and around the oven cavity. The circulating hot air penetrates food faster than the motionless air in a standard electric or gas oven—and food that heats faster tends to cook faster. That, in a nutshell, explains the physics of convection cooking.

Because of faster heating, many types of food can be cooked at temperatures somewhat lower than those suggested for standard ovens. The chart on pages 8 and 9 compares cooking temperatures and times for standard and convection ovens, thus showing where energy is saved, and where it is not.

CONVECTION BAKEWARE

Before making any recipe, check to see if the bakeware you intend to use fits into the oven. There's no reason to invest in new bakeware, as long as you have pans that fit. Since the point of convection cooking is to have hot air flowing around the food, be sure the bakeware leaves room for air circulation.

For example, if you plan to load a rack with several containers, leave airspace between the containers, as well as between the containers and the oven walls. Also, a baking sheet should not touch the walls of the oven. For recipes like oven-baked chicken parts, use a pan with low sides. High sides keep the hot air from circulating around the food.

While any type of bakeware works in a convection oven, aluminum or other metal pans convey heat fastest. We prefer metal pans for all kinds of convection baking. Further, dark or matte-finished bakeware bakes faster than shiny metal. We noticed that shiny copper took longer than enameled metal bakeware to cook the same dish. Stainless steel and

French tin also work well. Glass or ceramic containers slow down the cooking. If you use a bake-and-serve container with wooden handles, protect them with foil and be sure to fasten the foil firmly so it won't blow off.

TESTING, TESTING, ONE ... TWO ... THREE ...

Our first round of recipe testing involved cooking the same recipe in our countertop convection ovens and in a standard oven. We would like to share the results of these comparative tests because they reveal convection cooking's strengths.

Roasting refrigerated meat

For our first roasting test, we selected a marginally tender cut of beef that ordinarily would have been cooked with liquid as a pot roast. We took the 4½-pound roast straight from the refrigerator, inserted a meat thermometer, placed it in the convection oven without preheating, and set the temperature at 300° F. The roast reached an internal temperature of 135° F in 1 hour and 25 minutes (approximately 19 minutes per pound). We let the roast stand for 15 minutes before slicing it thinly. It was uniformly rare, exceptionally juicy, and surprisingly tender.

The same size roast cooked in a standard oven took 1 hour and 45 minutes (plus preheating time) at 325° F. We judged the convection oven roast to be somewhat juicier and more evenly rare. (See the recipe for boneless rump roast, page 12, if you want to duplicate this successful roast.)

KitchenAid ovens come with a special convection roasting rack that fits over the broiler drip pan.

Roasting frozen meat

Frankly, we were somewhat skeptical about putting a frozen chunk of meat in the oven without thawing it. But we were very pleased with the way a 4-pound 3-ounce sirloin tip roast looked and tasted after 2 hours and 10 minutes of convection cooking. After an hour of cooking, we inserted a thermometer and then removed the roast when its internal temperature reached 135° F. Except for the ends, the roast was evenly rare, juicy, and delicious.

The roasting chart on page 13 gives suggested times for roasting refrigerator-temperature meat and frozen meat. Naturally, cooking frozen meat uses more energy and takes more time.

Broiling

Convection broiling is actually high-temperature convection roasting. No preheating of the oven is required, and results are similar to those obtained when using a rotisserie. Convection broiling is suitable for thick cuts of meat, poultry, or fish. For best results, turn the food over halfway through the broiling process.

Poultry

We love the effect convection roasting has on chicken skin. Our first roast chicken came out a lovely golden brown with an appealingly crisp skin. Like the roast beef, it was juicier and more tender than chicken roasted in a standard oven. We roasted a 3½-pound chicken, breast side up, at a temperature of 350° F with no preheating (compared with 375° F in the standard oven with preheating). It reached an internal temperature of 185° F in 1 hour, compared with 1 hour and 30 minutes in the standard oven. (We do not recommend roasting poultry that is still frozen.)

Baking fish

Many people avoid baking fresh fish because of the smoke and smell. But convection baking eliminates that problem, even when the oven is set at very high temperatures. We convection baked a ¾-inch-thick fillet of red snapper at 450° F—the original recipe called for a preheated standard oven at 500° F. In both kinds of ovens, the fish cooked in 10 minutes, and both versions were tender and flavorful.

Baking egg dishes

Fluffy soufflés and creamy quiches baked splendidly in our tests. The soufflé was higher and lighter than an identical one baked in a standard oven. The reason beaten egg whites cause a soufflé (or any recipe) to rise higher when convection cooked is that the temperature is more constant than in most standard ovens. Though both kinds of ovens cycle on and off to maintain a temperature, the moving air in a convection oven sustains the temperature better than the motionless air in a standard oven.

Even quiche was puffier and better browned than the same quiche baked in a standard oven. The

time and temperature were virtually the same for both kinds of ovens.

Casseroles, stews & au gratin dishes

Convection cooking duplicated the standard oven's results for all the covered casserole recipes we tested. In most cases, the time and temperature were the same, too. Au gratin recipes, or any recipes that call for browning during baking, are improved by the convection oven's hot air method of cooking. To prevent overbrowning we baked uncovered casseroles about 25° lower than suggested in standard recipes.

Baking breads

We saved some energy by baking yeast bread at 325° F rather than 375° F in a standard oven, but the loaf took about the same amount of time to bake. The convection oven loaf came out higher than the standard oven loaf, though, and it had a better crust and an excellent texture.

Whole-menu baking

Another advantage of the convection oven is that you can bake a whole menu of recipes at the same time with no crossover of flavors. Moreover, everything will cook evenly. Just be sure to remember to allow at least an inch of space around the edges of baking sheets and to stagger pans at different levels for maximum air circulation. (For some suggested menus that can be baked all at one time, turn to page 42.)

Multilevel baking

We saved time and achieved good results when we baked on two or even three racks at the same time. Six pies (two on each rack staggered with the pies on the other two racks) browned nicely, cooked to even doneness, and received rave reviews, as did six loaves of bread baked at the same time on two racks. We used temperature settings 25° to 50° lower than in a standard oven; cooking time was the same or slightly longer than when baking on one rack in a standard oven.

(Continued on next page)

ADAPTING RECIPES FOR CONVECTION COOKING

"How do I adapt my favorite recipes for convection cooking?" That's everyone's first question. This chart shows how temperature and time for food cooked in a standard gas or electric oven compare with temperature and time for the same food prepared in a convection oven. Sometimes you'll note a saving in both energy and time. Sometimes the saving will be just in one or the other. Occasionally, there's no saving at all.

Use this chart as a guide when adapting standard recipes for convection cooking. You'll find more detailed charts on page 13 for roasting meat and on page 29 for roasting poultry.

Food	Standard oven temperature (Fahrenheit)	Time	Convection oven selection & temperature (Fahrenheit)	Time	How to adapt standard recipes for convection cooking
BEEF					
Rump roast, boneless, 4 pounds	325°	1¾ hours (rare)	Roast 300°	1¼ hours (rare)	Lower temperature 25° (but not lower than 300°). Figure ⅓ less time. Use meat thermometer (135°–140° F is rare). Let stand for 15 minutes before carving.
Sirloin tip, tied, 4 pounds	325°	2 hours (rare)	Roast 300°	1¼ hours (rare)	Lower temperature 25° (but not lower than 300°). Figure ⅓ less time. Use meat thermometer (135°–140° F is rare). Let stand for 15 minutes before carving.
T-bone steak, 1 inch thick, broiled	3 inches from heat	13–15 minutes (rare)	Broil 450°	16–18 minutes (rare)	Place on rack over drip pan. Figure 3–5 minutes more time.
Meat loaf, 2 pounds ground chuck, 5 by 9-inch loaf pan	350°	1 hour	Roast 325°	1–1¼ hours	Lower temperature 25°. Figure same time or slightly longer.
PORK					
Loin, boned and rolled, 3 pounds	325°	1½ hours	Roast 300°	1¼ hours	Lower temperature 25°. Figure about 25 minutes per pound. Use meat thermometer. Pork must reach 170° F to be done.
Loin, bone in, 3½ pounds	325°	2¼ hours	Roast 300°	2 hours	Same as above, but figure about 35 minutes per pound. Use meat thermometer. Pork must reach 170° F to be done.
Pork chops, ¾ inch thick, broiled	3 inches from heat	15–20 minutes	Broil 450°	20–25 minutes	Place on rack over drip pan. Figure 5–10 minutes more time.
Ham, fully cooked, 6 pounds	300°–325°	1½–2 hours	Roast 300°	1–1¾ hours	Time depends on shape and thickness.
LAMB					
Leg of lamb, 5–6 pounds	325°	2½ hours	Roast 300°	1¼–1¾ hours	Lower temperature 25°. Figure about 17 minutes per pound. Use meat thermometer (150°–155° F is medium).
Lamb chops, 1 inch thick, broiled	3 inches from heat	12 minutes (medium)	Broil 450°	14 minutes (medium)	Place on rack over drip pan. Figure about 2 minutes more time.
POULTRY					
Broiler-fryer, 3–4 pounds, roasted	375°	1½–2 hours	Roast 350°	1–1½ hours	Lower temperature 25°.
Broiler-fryer, quartered	375°	40–45 minutes	Roast 350°	40–45 minutes	Lower temperature 25°. Time is same.
Cornish hen, 12 ounces	425°	1 hour	Roast 375°	45 minutes	Lower temperature 50°.
Turkey, 10–16 pounds	325°	3–4½ hours	Roast 300°	2⅓–3 hours	Lower temperature 25°. Meat thermometer in thigh registers 170°–180° F when done. Let stand for 10–15 minutes before carving.
FISH					
Steaks or fillets, 2–3 pounds total, ½ inch thick	350°	20 minutes	Roast 350°	15–20 minutes	Keep temperature same. Test for doneness 10 minutes before recommended time.
Whole, 4½–5 pounds	400°	45 minutes	Roast 400°	30–40 minutes	Keep temperature same. Test for doneness 15 minutes before recommended time.

Food	Standard oven temperature (Fahrenheit)	Time	Convection oven selection & temperature (Fahrenheit)	Time	How to adapt standard recipes for convection cooking
VEGETABLES					
Potatoes, baked	425°	40–60 minutes	Roast 375°	40–50 minutes	Lower temperature 50°. Time is almost the same.
Potatoes, scalloped, 2-quart casserole	350°	1½–1¾ hours	Bake 325°	1½–1¾ hours	Lower temperature 25°. Time is same.
Acorn squash, halved	350°	1 hour	Bake 350°	40–50 minutes	Keep temperature same. Figure ⅓ less time.
Green bean casserole, 1½-quart	350°	35 minutes	Bake 300°–325°	40 minutes	Lower temperature for side dish to cook with meat. Add 5 minutes.
EGGS & CHEESE					
Quiche, 9-inch	350°	35–45 minutes	Bake 325°–350°	25–35 minutes	Keep temperature same or lower it 25°. Figure 10 minutes less time.
Soufflé, cheese, 2-quart	350°	35 minutes	Bake 350°	27 minutes	Keep temperature same. Time is almost the same. Test for doneness 5–10 minutes before recommended time. Check for browning.
CASSEROLES					
Macaroni and cheese, 1½-quart casserole	350°	35–40 minutes	Bake 325°	35–40 minutes	Lower temperature 25°. Time is same.
Tuna noodle casserole, 2-quart	375°	30 minutes	Bake 350°	30–40 minutes	Lower temperature 25°. Time is same or slightly longer.
Tamale pie, 3-quart shallow pan	350°	40 minutes	Bake 325°	40–45 minutes	Lower temperature 25°. Time is same or slightly longer.
BREADS					
Plain yeast loaves, 5 by 9-inch loaf pan	375°	50 minutes	Roast 325°; rack 1	30–40 minutes	Lower temperature 50°. Figure 10–20 minutes less time. Check for browning.
4 to 6 yeast loaves, 5 by 9-inch loaf pan	*	*	Bake 300°	40–50 minutes	Convection cooking offers even browning for multilevel baking, unlike standard ovens.
Fruit and nut quick bread, 5 by 9-inch loaf pan	350°	45–60 minutes	Bake 300°	1 hour, 10 minutes	Lower temperature 50°. Figure 25–40 minutes more time.
Popovers	400°	40 minutes	Bake 350°	40–45 minutes	Lower temperature 50°. Time is same or slightly longer. Check for browning.
Cornbread, 9 by 9-inch pan	425°	20–25 minutes	Bake 350°	25–30 minutes	Lower temperature 75°. Figure 5–10 minutes more time. Check for browning.
Biscuits, baking powder	450°	12 minutes	Bake 375°	20–30 minutes	Lower temperature 75°. Figure 8–18 minutes more time.
DESSERTS					
Butter cakes, 2 layers, 8-inch round pans	350°	40 minutes	Bake 275°	45–55 minutes	Lower temperature 75°. Figure 5–15 minutes more time.
Angel food cake, 10-inch tube pan	375°	35–40 minutes	Roast 300°; rack 1	40–45 minutes	Lower temperature 75°. Figure 5–15 minutes more time. Check for browning.
Pound cake, 5 by 9-inch loaf pan	325°	1 hour	Bake 275°	1¼–1½ hours	Lower temperature 50°. Figure 15–30 minutes more time.
Drop cookies, 1 sheet standard oven, 1–3 sheets convection oven	350°	8–10 minutes	Bake 300°	8–10 minutes	Lower temperature 50°. Time is same.
Refrigerator cookies, 1 sheet standard oven, 1–3 sheets convection oven	400°	10–12 minutes	Bake 350°	10–12 minutes	Lower temperature 50°. Time is same.
2-crust fruit pie, 9-inch pan	375°	50 minutes	Bake 350°	50 minutes	Lower temperature 25°. Time is same.
Cream puffs	400°	25–30 minutes	Bake 325°	25–30 minutes	Lower temperature 75°. Time is same.
Cake mixes, 2 layers, 8-inch round pans	350°	30–35 minutes	Bake 275°	40–45 minutes	Lower temperature 75°. Figure 10–15 minutes more time.
FROZEN CONVENIENCE FOODS					
Pizza, 12-inch	425°	15–18 minutes	Roast 425°	15–18 minutes	Temperature and time are same.
Berry pie, 9-inch pan	400°	45–50 minutes	Roast 350°	50–60 minutes	Lower temperature 50°. Figure 5–10 minutes more time. Check for browning.

*Not recommended for standard oven

Wreathed by mandarin orange slices, sautéed onions, cashews, and watercress, this succulent pork roast makes a picture-perfect entrée. The recipe for citrus pork roast with onions is on page 21.

Meats

Whether your menu calls for hamburgers baked on French rolls or a spectacular beef roast cloaked in a golden crust of brioche, you can count on convection cooking for delicious meat entrées.

We tested a variety of meats—from large cuts of beef, veal, pork, and lamb to ground meats and chops. In this chapter you'll find the best of our testing. We experimented with dry-heat cooking (roasting and broiling) as well as with moist-heat cooking (casseroles and stews). Only one method gave us pause, and that was broiling. Convection broiling is really high-temperature roasting. Results are similar to those obtained when using a rotisserie.

Roast meats were marvelous. The hot air seals in meat juices, and because a roast can be placed directly on the special convection roasting rack, the constantly circulating hot air reaches all sides. Also, you can roast a large cut of meat at a lower temperature for a shorter length of time than in a standard oven.

We used a 300° F oven temperature for test-roasting, and it gave consistently good results with little shrinkage. To determine roasting times, we used meat directly from the refrigerator and we didn't preheat the oven. Individual ovens vary, though, and you may prefer your meat done more or less than suggested in the recipes, so be sure to use a reliable meat thermometer. At today's meat prices, such a thermometer is a good investment—you can be certain a roast is done to your liking and that every bite will be worth its price.

Remember that a roast continues to cook for 10 to 15 minutes after you take it from the oven, so the meat's internal temperature will increase 10° to 15°. Obviously, then, a 10 to 15-minute standing period is important; it completes the cooking and also makes the roast easier to carve. (See the roasting chart on page 13.)

Roasting isn't the only cooking method we used for meats, though. In this chapter we also include recipes for savory oven stews, meat loaves, casseroles, and slow-cooked meats.

Adapting your own recipes. The recommended temperature for roasting meats in a gas or electric oven is usually 325° F. When you use a convection oven, just lower the recommended temperature by 25°. You needn't preheat the oven. Follow the roasting chart on page 13 for time and internal temperature for meats.

For covered dishes like stews or moist-cooked meats, use the same temperature and time suggested in your favorite recipe, but check your meat to see if it's done about 10 to 15 minutes before the recommended time is up. Again, no preheating is necessary. For uncovered meat casseroles or meat pies, lower the recommended oven temperature 25° to prevent overbrowning. Meat loaf is also convection baked 25° lower than standard recipes indicate, so it won't get too brown; you may have to increase the cooking time by 15 minutes or so, though.

Slow cooking is another convection-oven option. For directions and recipes for slow-cooked meats, see page 24.

SUCCULENT OVEN RUMP ROAST

Here is a cut of beef generally pot roasted, yet it can also be cooked in a convection oven without liquid. The result is a lean, yet juicy and tender roast. This roast is most tender if cooked just to the rare stage.

1 teaspoon <u>each</u> salt and dry mustard
¼ teaspoon pepper
4 to 5-pound boneless beef rump roast

Mix together salt, mustard, and pepper; rub mixture over roast. Place meat, uncovered and fat side up, on rack over convection oven drip pan. Roast in 300° convection oven for 18 to 20 minutes per pound or until a meat thermometer inserted in center registers 135° for rare. Remove to a carving board, cover lightly with foil, and let stand for 10 to 15 minutes before slicing. Carve in thin slices. Makes 6 to 8 servings.

BEEF ROAST IN BRIOCHE

A rolled beef roast encased in a golden crust makes an elegant presentation for a company meal. Each step—roasting the meat, preparing the buttery, yeast dough, and making the wine-scented sauce—can be done a day in advance. The next morning, you can assemble the roast in the pastry and deco-

rate it, leaving only the final baking for the big occasion.

3 to 4-pound rolled, boneless beef roast (such as sirloin tip or rib eye)
Mushroom filling (recipe follows)
Vegetable-wine sauce (recipe follows)
1 package active dry yeast
½ cup warm water (about 110°)
4 teaspoons sugar
½ cup (¼ lb.) butter or margarine, softened
3 eggs
¾ teaspoon salt
2¾ to 3 cups all-purpose flour
1 egg yolk, beaten with 2 tablespoons milk

Place roast, uncovered, on rack over convection oven drip pan. Roast in 300° convection oven for 18 to 25 minutes per pound or until a meat thermometer inserted in center registers 135° for rare. Let roast cool at room temperature for at least 1 hour. Skim fat from pan drippings, if necessary; reserve drippings for vegetable-wine sauce. Cut strings from roast, trim off all fat, cover, and chill overnight.

Meanwhile, prepare mushroom filling and vegetable-wine sauce.

For the brioche, combine yeast, water, and 1 teaspoon of the sugar in a measuring cup; let stand until bubbly (about 10 minutes).

In a large bowl, beat butter with remaining 3 teaspoons sugar until creamy. Beat in yeast mixture, eggs, salt, and ¾ cup of the flour. Gradually beat in 2 cups more flour. Turn dough out on a lightly floured board and knead just until smooth (about 3 minutes); dough should be soft. Place dough in a greased bowl; cover and let rise in a warm place until doubled (1¼ to 1½ hours). Punch dough down;

cover and refrigerate for at least 6 hours or until next day.

One hour before wrapping in dough, remove roast from refrigerator. With a tape measure or piece of string, measure circumference of roast at thickest point; also measure length. Turn dough onto a lightly floured board and roll out to make a ¼-inch-thick rectangle at least 2 inches longer than circumference of roast, and 2 inches wider than length. With a sharp knife, trim rectangle to 2 inches more than roast measures; reserve trimmings for decoration.

Spread a 4-inch-wide strip of mushroom filling down center of dough and set meat on filling. Brush edges of dough with part of the egg yolk mixture and wrap dough around roast, pinching edges together firmly. Gently place wrapped roast, seam side down, on a greased baking sheet. Brush all over with egg mixture. Cut dough scraps into decorative shapes and set on top of roast; do not brush decoration with egg. Refrigerate for at least 20 minutes or as long as 3 hours.

Bake in preheated 300° convection oven for 1¼ to 1½ hours or until crust is richly browned. Insert a meat thermometer through brioche into thickest part of roast. Meat is hot when thermometer registers about 120°. Meanwhile, place sauce over medium heat and, stirring occasionally, bring to a boil.

To serve, place roast in brioche on a serving platter and let stand for 10 minutes. With a serrated knife, cut into ¾-inch-thick slices. Pass vegetable-wine sauce to spoon over individual servings. Makes 8 to 10 servings.

Mushroom filling. In a wide frying pan over medium-high heat, melt ¼ cup (4 tablespoons) **butter** or margarine. Add 1 pound **mushrooms** (chopped), ½ cup chopped **green onions** (including tops), 2 teaspoons **Dijon mustard** (op-

(Continued on page 14)

ROASTING MEAT

Cut of meat	Convection roasting temperature (Fahrenheit)	Minutes per pound, refrigerated	Minutes per pound, frozen	Internal temperature when done (Fahrenheit)
BEEF				
Rolled rib eye, boneless, 3–5 pounds	300°	Rare: 18–25 Medium: 28–29 Well: 30–31	Rare: 33–35 Medium: 38–39 Well: 40–41	Rare: 135°–140° Medium: 160° Well: 170°
Standing rib, 6–7 pounds	300°	Rare: 20–22 Medium: 25–28 Well: 28–30	Rare: 30–32 Medium: 35–38 Well: 38–40	Rare: 135°–140° Medium: 160° Well: 170°
Rump roast, boneless, 4–6 pounds	300°	Rare: 18–20 Medium: 21–24 Well: 26–30	Rare: 29–34 Medium: 35–40 Well: 41–46	Rare: 135°–140° Medium: 160° Well: 170°
PORK				
Loin, 3–4 pounds	300°	Well: 33–35	Well: 46–50	Well: 170°
Shoulder, 4–5 pounds	300°	Well: 28–30	Well: 41–45	Well: 180°
Ham, fully cooked				
5 pounds	300°	13–14	—	130°
9 pounds	300°	10–11	—	130°
LAMB				
Leg, whole, 6–8 pounds	300°	Rare: 16 Medium: 17 Well: 25–27	Rare: 26 Medium: 27 Well: 35–37	Rare: 140° Medium: 150°–155° Well: 180°
VEAL				
Loin, 3–4 pounds	300°	Well: 20–23	Well: 30–33	Well: 170°
Shoulder, 5–6 pounds	300°	Well: 28–30	Well: 38–40	Well: 170°

BROILING MEAT & CHICKEN

Cut of meat	Offset rack position	Convection broil temperature (Fahrenheit)	Minutes per pound, refrigerated
BEEF			
Steak, 1 inch thick	2	450°	Rare: 16–18 Medium: 19–21 Well: 22–24
Steak, 1½ inches thick	2	450°	Rare: 20–22 Medium: 24–26 Well: 34–38
PORK			
Pork chops, 1 inch thick	2	450°	Well: 23–25
LAMB			
Lamb chops, 1 inch thick	2	450°	Medium: 13–15
CHICKEN			
Chicken pieces	2	350°	Well: 31–33

tional), and ¼ cup **Madeira** or dry sherry. Cook, stirring occasionally, until mushrooms are soft. Raise heat to high and cook, stirring constantly, until all liquid evaporates. Cool, cover, and refrigerate.

Vegetable-wine sauce. In a 2-quart saucepan over medium heat, melt 3 tablespoons **butter** or margarine. Add 1 cup each chopped **carrots** and **onions** and cook, stirring, until onion is soft. Add ¼ teaspoon **thyme leaves**; 1 can (14 oz.) **beef broth**; ⅓ cup **Madeira**, dry sherry, or tawny port; reserved **meat drippings**; and ½ to 1 teaspoon **bottled brown gravy sauce** (optional). Cover and simmer for 5 minutes; whirl in a blender until smooth. Add **salt** and **pepper** to taste; then stir in 1 teaspoon **cornstarch** mixed with 1 teaspoon **water**; cover and refrigerate.

ORANGE-THYME BEEF ROAST

A citrus and herb marinade flavors and forms a light sauce for this handsome beef roast. You might bake potatoes along with the meat for about the last hour.

    4½ to 5-pound rolled, boneless beef roast (such as sirloin tip, top round, or cross rib)
⅓ cup each red wine vinegar and salad oil
1½ teaspoons grated orange peel
½ teaspoon thyme leaves
1 medium-size orange, cut in half, or ½ cup orange juice
    Salt

Place roast in a deep bowl or heavy plastic bag. In a measuring cup, combine vinegar, salad oil, orange peel, and thyme; pour over meat. Cover or seal

and refrigerate for 4 hours or until next day; turn meat occasionally in marinade.

Lift meat from marinade; reserve liquid. Place meat, uncovered, on rack over convection oven drip pan. Roast in 300° convection oven, basting meat occasionally with marinade, for 18 to 25 minutes per pound or until a meat thermometer inserted in center registers 135° for rare. Remove to a carving board, cover lightly with foil, and let stand for 10 to 15 minutes before slicing.

Meanwhile, skim and discard fat from pan drippings; squeeze juice from orange into pan drippings. Accompany sliced beef with pan juices. Season beef and juices with salt to taste. Makes 8 to 10 servings.

CROSS RIB WITH ITALIAN ROASTED VEGETABLES

A handsome beef roast cooked with potatoes, onions, carrots, garlic, and herbs makes a fine dinner for a special occasion.

½ cup olive oil or salad oil
¾ teaspoon oregano leaves
½ teaspoon thyme leaves
1 clove garlic, slivered
2 pounds (about 6) red new potatoes (¾-inch-wide strip peeled around centers)
3 medium onions, peeled, cut into sixths
6 to 8 medium-size carrots
    4½ to 5-pound cross rib beef roast (boneless rolled chuck)
    Chopped parsley for garnish

Pour oil into convection oven roasting pan; mix in oregano, thyme, and garlic. Add vegetables, turning to coat with oil mixture. Place roast, fat side up, on rack over convection oven

drip pan with vegetables, or in center of vegetables. Roast, uncovered, in 300° convection oven for 18 to 25 minutes per pound, 1½ to 2 hours in all, or until meat thermometer inserted in center registers 135° for rare and vegetables are tender. Turn vegetables after 1 hour. When done, transfer roast to a carving board, cover lightly with foil, and let stand for 10 to 15 minutes before slicing.

Carve roast in thin slices. Serve surrounded by vegetables, drizzling them lightly with oil mixture and sprinkling with parsley. Makes 8 to 10 servings.

OVEN-BROWNED BEEF STEW

Pictured on page 15

This stew is particularly fast to assemble for the convection oven, as the meat needs no browning.

5 whole cloves
16 small onions (same size as meat pieces)
2 pounds boneless beef stew meat, cut into 1½-inch cubes
2 tablespoons sugar
1 cup hot water
1½ teaspoons salt
½ teaspoon bottled brown gravy sauce
1 tablespoon red wine vinegar
1 bay leaf
⅛ teaspoon thyme leaves
2 tablespoons flour mixed with 2 tablespoons water
    Chopped parsley for garnish

Stick cloves into 5 of the onions. (Onions should be same size as meat cubes; if using larger onions, cut into halves or quarters.) In a greased 2-quart baking pan, alternate meat pieces and onions.

(Continued on page 16)

Let the rich aroma of an old-fashioned oven-browned beef stew (recipe on facing page) beckon your family to dinner. While the stew browns in the convection oven, you can also bake a side dish, such as potatoes gratin (recipe on page 51), for maximum oven use.

In a small frying pan over medium heat, melt sugar and stir until caramelized to a dark golden brown (do not burn); remove from heat. Carefully and gradually add the 1 cup hot water (sugar will harden); then return to heat and stir until sugar melts again. Stir in salt, gravy sauce, vinegar, bay leaf, and thyme; pour over meat.

Bake, covered, in 300° convection oven, stirring once or twice, for 2½ to 3 hours or until meat is tender when pierced. About 10 to 15 minutes before serving, remove pan from oven and stir flour mixture into meat gravy. Return pan to oven and continue to bake, uncovered, until thickened. Stir well and serve sprinkled with parsley. Makes about 6 servings.

OVEN-BAKED CORNED BEEF

As this moist, tender corned beef cooks in a convection oven it makes its own flavorful liquid. For an easy buffet supper for 8 to 10 people, serve it sliced, warm or cold. Provide an assortment of bagels, with butter, mustard, and sweet pickles, so guests can create their own sandwiches. You can round out the buffet with a carrot and raisin salad.

4½ to 5-pound bottom round corned beef
1   **small orange**

Trim and discard some (but not all) fat from corned beef. Rinse meat well under running water and place in a 6-quart Dutch oven or pan. Cover corned beef with water; cover pan and refrigerate for at least 4 hours or until next day. Pour out and discard soaking liquid.

Cut off and discard ends of orange; cut orange crosswise into thin slices. Place slices on and around meat, cover pan, and bake in 300° convection oven for 3½ to 4 hours or until meat is tender when pierced.

Lift meat from juices. Slice and serve hot; or cool, cover, and refrigerate for at least 4 hours. Cut into thin slices for sandwiches. Makes 8 to 10 servings.

BARBECUE-STYLE SWISS STEAK

Always a family favorite, Swiss steak is never easier or more tender than when it's oven-simmered in a zesty barbecue sauce. You might accompany it with noodles cooked in beef broth.

2 pounds boneless bottom round steak, cut ¾ inch thick
Salt
Pepper
2   **tablespoons all-purpose flour**
    About 2 tablespoons salad oil
2   **large onions, sliced**
1   **envelope instant onion soup mix (for individual serving)**
1   **clove garlic, minced or pressed**
½   **cup tomato-based chili sauce or catsup**
¾   **cup water**
2   **tablespoons lemon juice**
1   **teaspoon each Worcestershire and Dijon mustard**

Trim and discard fat from meat; cut meat into 4 to 6 serving-size pieces. Lay pieces on cutting board; sprinkle meat with salt, pepper, and 1 tablespoon of the flour. With a mallet or edge of a saucer, pound flour into meat. Turn pieces over; sprinkle with salt, pepper, and remaining 1 tablespoon flour, then pound again. Heat oil in a 4-quart Dutch oven over medium heat. Add meat, a few pieces at a time, and brown well on both sides; remove meat as it browns. Add more salad oil, if needed.

To same pan, add onions and cook, stirring often, until soft. Return meat to pan. In a bowl, combine onion soup mix, garlic, chili sauce, water, lemon juice, Worcestershire, and mustard; pour over meat. Bake, covered, in 300° convection oven for about 2 hours or until meat is tender when pierced. Transfer meat to a serving dish. Skim and discard fat from cooking sauce; then spoon onions and sauce over meat. Makes 4 to 6 servings.

BURGUNDY BEEF SHANKS

Baked potatoes make excellent partners for these moist and tender beef shanks—and they can bake in the same oven for the last 45 minutes.

4   **slices beef shank, about 1½ inches thick (3 to 4 lbs. total)**
    All-purpose flour
1   **tablespoon salad oil or olive oil**
1   **large onion, finely chopped**
1   **carrot, chopped**
1   **teaspoon salt**
½   **teaspoon thyme leaves**
1   **cup beef broth**
1   **can (8 oz.) tomato sauce**
¼   **cup dry red wine**

Dust meat lightly with flour. Heat oil in a large frying pan over medium heat. Add meat and brown on both sides; transfer to a 4-quart baking pan. Cook onion in pan drippings until lightly browned; stir in carrot, salt, thyme, broth, tomato sauce, and wine. Pour vegetable mixture over meat. Bake, covered, in 350° convection oven for 2 to 2½ hours or until meat is tender when pierced. Transfer meat to a warm serving dish. Skim and discard fat from sauce, then spoon sauce over meat. Makes 4 servings.

SHORT RIBS WITH NOODLES

For this flavorful main dish, you can do all the cooking—including browning the meat and simmering the noodles—in your convection oven.

- 3 **pounds beef short ribs, cut in serving-size pieces**
- ¼ **cup all-purpose flour**
- 1 **teaspoon salt**
- ¼ **teaspoon pepper**
- 2 **cups hot water**
- 1 **envelope (1⅜ oz.) dry onion soup mix**
- 6 **ounces packaged noodles (twisted or plain)**
  Chopped parsley for garnish

Cut away excess fat from the meat; discard fat. Combine flour, salt, and pepper. Coat each meat piece on all sides with flour mixture; shake off excess flour. Arrange ribs, slightly apart, in a 9-inch-square baking pan or deep 3½ to 4-quart Dutch oven. Bake, uncovered, in 450° convection oven for 30 minutes. Remove from oven and reduce convection oven temperature to 300°. Spoon off and discard fat from pan juices; stir water and soup mix into pan. Cover pan tightly and bake for about 2 hours or until meat is tender when pierced.

Remove pan from oven; skim off fat. Stir noodles into liquid in pan. Cover pan again, return to oven, and cook for 15 more minutes. Stir, add a little more water if needed, then cook 10 to 15 minutes longer or until noodles are tender. Sprinkle with parsley just before serving. Makes 4 to 6 servings.

BEEF & BISCUIT CASSEROLE

Crisp, tender homemade biscuits top this rich, red stew. Accompany it with steamed broccoli spears.

- 2½ **pounds boneless beef chuck, trimmed of fat**
- 2 **tablespoons salad oil**
- 1 **large onion, chopped**
- ⅓ **pound mushrooms, sliced**
- 1 **can (14½ oz.) tomatoes**
- ½ **cup water**
- 1 **can (6 oz.) tomato paste**
- 1 **tablespoon sugar**
- 1½ **teaspoons salt**
- ½ **teaspoon each pepper and Worcestershire**
- 1 **tablespoon flour**
- ¾ **cup sour cream**
  Sour cream biscuits (recipe follows)

Cut beef into strips ½ inch wide, ½ inch thick, and 2 inches long. Heat salad oil in a large, heavy frying pan or in a Dutch oven over medium-high heat. Add about half the beef strips and cook, turning, until browned. Remove and set aside browned meat and cook remaining half, adding more oil if needed. Remove browned meat and set aside. Add onion and mushrooms to pan; reduce heat to medium and cook, stirring, until onions are soft. Return meat to pan; add tomatoes, including juice (break up tomatoes with a spoon), water, tomato paste,

sugar, salt, pepper, and Worcestershire; bring to a boil. Spread beef mixture in a shallow 2½ to 3-quart baking pan. Bake, covered, in 300° convection oven for 2 to 2½ hours or until beef is tender when pierced.

Remove stew from oven. Raise convection oven temperature to 375°. Stir flour into sour cream until blended; stir into hot stew. Top stew with biscuits. Return stew to oven and bake, uncovered, for 25 to 30 more minutes or until biscuits are well browned. Makes 6 to 8 servings.

Sour cream biscuits. Stir together 1¾ cups **all-purpose flour**, 2 teaspoons **baking powder**, and ½ teaspoon **salt**. With a pastry blender or 2 knives, cut ½ cup **shortening** into flour mixture until fine crumbs form. Stir in ¾ cup **sour cream** until blended. Knead dough lightly on a floured board, then pat dough out to ½-inch thickness. Cut dough in about 2-inch rounds. Makes about 12 biscuits.

GRATED CARROT MEAT LOAF

A mustard-accented glaze enlivens this moist, carrot-flecked meat loaf. It makes a good oven meal with potatoes and a green bean casserole (page 48).

- 3 **eggs**
- ½ **cup milk**
- 1½ **cups soft bread crumbs**
- 2 **pounds ground beef chuck**
- 2 **medium carrots, shredded**
- 2 **tablespoons prepared horseradish**
- 1 **envelope (1⅜ oz.) dry onion soup mix**
  Topping (recipe follows)

In a large mixing bowl, beat eggs and milk; add bread crumbs and let stand for 5 minutes. Mix in ground beef, carrots,

(Continued on page 19)

Giant-size hot sandwiches can satisfy giant-size appetites—
especially when they're made with a mixture of ground beef,
Swiss cheese, onions, and mushrooms baked on crisp
French rolls. The recipe for oven-baked hamburgers is
on the facing page.

horseradish, and soup mix. Pat into a 5 by 9-inch loaf pan. Spread topping evenly over meat mixture. Bake, uncovered, in 325° convection oven for 1 to 1¼ hours or until well browned. Spoon off fat. Let stand for about 5 minutes before slicing. Makes 8 to 10 servings.

Topping. In a small bowl, combine ¼ cup **catsup**, 3 tablespoons **brown sugar**, and 2 tablespoons **Dijon mustard.**

VEGETABLE MEAT LOAF SQUARES

This novel meat loaf, frosted with melted cheese, contains a surprise layer of fresh vegetables.

3   tablespoons butter or margarine
¾   cup each finely diced carrots, potatoes, onions, and celery
2   teaspoons dry basil
1½ teaspoons salt
½   teaspoon pepper
2   pounds lean ground beef
1   egg
¼   cup each fine dry bread crumbs and chopped parsley
¼   teaspoon garlic powder
½   cup shredded jack cheese

In a wide frying pan over medium heat, melt butter. Add carrots, potatoes, onions, and celery and cook, stirring often, until vegetables are tender. Combine basil, salt, and pepper; stir half the seasoning mixture into vegetable mixture. Remove pan from heat and set aside.

In a bowl, mix together ground beef, egg, crumbs, parsley, garlic powder, and the remaining half of the seasoning mixture. Pat half the meat mixture into the bottom and up the sides of a 7 by 11-inch baking pan.

Spread vegetables on top; cover evenly with remaining meat mixture.

Bake, uncovered, in 350° convection oven for 30 to 35 minutes or until well browned. Sprinkle with cheese and bake for 3 to 5 more minutes or until cheese melts. Let stand for about 10 minutes, then cut into squares. Makes 6 to 8 servings.

BEEF & SPINACH SUPPER PIE

Almost a meal in itself, this colorful ground beef pie needs only the complement of a crisp cabbage salad. Add fresh wedges of oranges or tangerines for dessert.

Pastry for single-crust 9-inch pie
Flour
1   tablespoon salad oil
1   medium-size onion, chopped
1   medium-size green pepper, seeded and chopped
1   clove garlic, minced or pressed
1   pound lean ground beef
1   teaspoon each salt and oregano leaves
¼   teaspoon pepper
½   teaspoon each dry basil and marjoram leaves
¼   cup catsup
1   package (10 oz.) frozen chopped spinach, thawed
3   eggs, lightly beaten
2   cups (8 oz.) shredded sharp Cheddar cheese
1   large, firm, ripe tomato, sliced

Roll out pastry on a lightly floured board, then fit into a 9-inch pie pan. Flute edge and set aside.

Heat oil in a wide frying pan over medium heat. Add onion, green pepper, and garlic; cook

until vegetables are soft. Crumble in beef and cook, stirring, until meat is no longer pink. Spoon off and discard fat, then stir in salt, oregano, pepper, basil, marjoram, and catsup.

Squeeze moisture from spinach; stir spinach into meat. Remove pan from heat and cool slightly; then stir in eggs and 1 cup of the cheese.

Spoon filling into unbaked shell. Bake in preheated 350° convection oven for 25 to 30 minutes or just until knife inserted in center comes out clean. Remove pie from oven, arrange tomato slices on top, and sprinkle evenly with remaining 1 cup cheese. Return to oven and bake for 5 more minutes or until cheese melts. Let pie stand for about 5 minutes before cutting in wedges. Makes 4 to 6 servings.

OVEN-BAKED HAMBURGERS

Pictured on page 18

Swiss cheese melts into ground-beef-and-mushroom patties as they bake atop crusty French rolls. Serve these sandwiches with your favorite coleslaw.

4   French rolls (3 by 5 inches each)
    Softened butter or margarine
3   tablespoons butter or margarine
2   green onions (including tops), finely chopped
¼   pound mushrooms, sliced
1   pound ground beef chuck
½   teaspoon each salt and garlic salt
1½ cups (6 oz.) shredded Swiss cheese

Cut rolls in half lengthwise; spread cut surfaces lightly with softened butter. Place in single layer, buttered sides up, on rack in 450° convection oven for 12 to

15 minutes or until crisp and lightly browned.

Meanwhile, in a wide frying pan over medium heat, melt the 3 tablespoons butter. Add onions and mushrooms and cook, just until glazed. Remove from heat and cool. Mix in ground beef, salt, garlic salt, and cheese.

Set aside tops of rolls. Pat the meat mixture on bottoms, covering to edges. Place meat-covered rolls on rack over convection oven roasting pan. Bake, uncovered, in 350° convection oven for 15 to 20 minutes or until well browned. Reheat roll tops in oven during the last 3 minutes. Makes 4 servings.

REUBEN PIE

Inspired by the popular Reuben sandwich, this meat pie has a "crust" of ground meat and a filling of sauerkraut and Swiss cheese. To complete the menu, add a mixed green salad, hot crusty rolls with butter, and beer.

- 1 pound lean ground beef
- ¼ pound lean ground pork or additional ground beef
- ⅓ cup rolled oats
- ¼ cup Worcestershire
- 1 egg
- ¼ teaspoon each pepper and garlic powder
- 1 can (16 oz.) sauerkraut, well drained
- 2 cups (8 oz.) shredded Swiss cheese
- 1½ teaspoons caraway seeds
- 1 can (3 oz.) French-fried onions
  Chili sauce or catsup

In a bowl, combine ground beef, pork, oats, Worcestershire, egg, pepper, and garlic powder. Turn mixture into a 9-inch pie pan and pat evenly into bottom and up sides. Bake, uncovered, in 325° convection oven for 15

minutes. Remove from oven and drain off accumulated liquid.

Meanwhile, in a bowl, combine sauerkraut, cheese, caraway seeds, and a fourth of the onions. Spoon into drained meat crust and return pie to oven for 15 minutes or until cheese is thoroughly melted. Sprinkle remaining onions over pie and continue to bake for 3 to 5 more minutes or until onions are warmed.

Cut into wedges to serve; pass chili sauce to spoon over individual portions. Makes 4 to 6 servings.

FIESTA TAMALE PIE

This cornmeal-crusted meat and vegetable casserole adapts perfectly to convection oven baking.

- 2 tablespoons salad oil
- 1 medium-size onion, chopped
- 1 clove garlic, minced or pressed
- 1 pound lean ground beef
- ½ pound bulk pork sausage
- 1 can (28 oz.) tomatoes
- 1 can (1 lb.) whole kernel corn, drained
- 1 tablespoon chili powder
- ½ teaspoon each salt, oregano leaves, and ground cumin
- 1 cup pitted ripe olives, drained
  Cornmeal topping (recipe follows)
- 1½ cups (6 oz.) shredded Cheddar cheese

Heat oil in a wide frying pan over medium heat; add onion and garlic and cook until onion is soft. Crumble in beef and sausage and cook until browned; spoon off and discard excess fat. Stir in tomatoes (break up with a spoon) and their liquid, corn, chili powder,

salt, oregano, and cumin. Simmer, uncovered, for 10 minutes, then stir in olives.

Spread mixture in a shallow 3-quart baking pan. Prepare topping and spoon over meat mixture, then sprinkle with cheese. Bake, uncovered, in preheated 300° convection oven for 40 to 45 minutes or until top is well browned and center feels firm when lightly touched. Makes 6 servings.

Cornmeal topping. In a medium-size bowl, beat 2 **eggs,** then beat in 1 cup each **milk** and **cornmeal.**

HAM LOAF WITH SWEET & SOUR GLAZE

Serve this moist, golden-glazed ham loaf for a family meal or buffet dinner. It goes very well with the sweet potato casserole on page 51.

- 2 eggs
- ½ cup sour cream
- 1 teaspoon each curry powder, ground ginger, and dry mustard
  Dash each paprika and ground nutmeg
- 1 cup soft bread crumbs
- 1 pound each ground pork and ground ham
  Sweet and sour glaze (recipe follows)
- 1 can (9 oz.) pineapple slices, drained and cut in halves
  Parsley sprigs for garnish

In a large bowl, beat together eggs, sour cream, curry, ginger, mustard, paprika, and nutmeg. Mix in bread crumbs, then ground pork and ham. Pat mixture into 4½ by 8½-inch loaf pan. Smooth surface of loaf and bake, uncovered, in 325° convection oven for 45 minutes.

Meanwhile, prepare sweet and sour glaze. Remove loaf from oven and drain off excess fat. Pour half the glaze over loaf and bake for 20 more minutes or until well browned. Remove loaf from oven and pour remaining glaze over loaf; let stand for 5 minutes. Remove loaf from pan and place on a serving platter. Decorate with pineapple and garnish with parsley. Makes 6 servings.

Sweet and sour glaze. In a small pan over medium heat, mix together ¼ cup **water**, ½ cup **cider vinegar**, 1 tablespoon **lemon juice**, and ½ cup firmly packed **brown sugar**. Bring mixture to a boil, then reduce heat and simmer uncovered for 15 minutes.

PORK LOIN WITH CHUTNEY GLAZE

Richly browned and crusty, this appealing pork roast is accented by a savory chutney glaze and accompanied by lime-drizzled papaya slices.

3 to 3½-pound pork loin roast	
3	tablespoons frozen orange juice concentrate, thawed
½	cup Major Grey chutney
2	tablespoons soy sauce
½	teaspoon <u>each</u> garlic salt and ground ginger
1	papaya
1	lime, cut in wedges

Place pork loin roast, fat side up and uncovered, on rack over convection oven roasting pan. Roast in 300° convection oven for 45 minutes. Meanwhile, in a blender or food processor combine orange juice concentrate, chutney, soy, garlic salt, and ginger; purée until smooth. Remove meat from oven, spoon half the sauce over meat, and roast for 30 more minutes. Remove from oven again, spoon remaining sauce over meat, and roast until a meat thermometer inserted in center of roast registers 170° (allow about 35 minutes per pound in all).

Transfer roast to a carving board. Peel papaya, halve, remove seeds, and slice. Carve roast and arrange in center of platter. Arrange papaya slices and lime wedges around roast. Makes 6 to 8 servings.

CITRUS PORK ROAST WITH ONIONS

Pictured on page 10

A succulent pork roast, garnished with sautéed onions, mandarin orange segments, and cashews, makes a handsome centerpiece for a company meal. The pork marinates first in wine and orange juice; then the marinade is used as a baste. The menu might also include a tart butter lettuce salad, baked or boiled new potatoes, and crisp snow peas.

	Citrus pork marinade (recipe follows)
	2½ to 3-pound boned, rolled pork loin roast
¼	cup butter or margarine
3	large onions, sliced
	Pork-citrus gravy (recipe follows)
1	can (11 oz.) mandarin orange segments (drained) or 2 or 3 fresh mandarins or tangerines (peeled, segmented, and seeded)
⅓	cup dry roasted cashews
	Watercress or parsley sprigs for garnish

Prepare citrus pork marinade. Place pork in a shallow dish and pour marinade over pork. Cover and refrigerate, turning roast occasionally to marinate evenly, for at least 8 hours or until next day.

Place roast, fat side up and uncovered, on rack over convection oven roasting pan. Roast in 300° convection oven, basting meat occasionally with some of remaining marinade, for about 25 minutes per pound or until a meat thermometer inserted into center of roast registers 170°.

About 45 minutes before roast is done, melt butter in a wide frying pan over medium heat. Add onions and cook, stirring often, for about 40 minutes or until golden; cover, reduce heat to low, and keep warm until ready to serve.

When pork is done, transfer it to a carving board, cover lightly, and set aside while you prepare pork-citrus gravy.

Carve pork in thin slices and arrange in center of a large platter. Spoon onions around pork. In drippings in which onions were cooked, lightly stir mandarin orange segments and cashews over low heat until warm; sprinkle mixture over onions. Garnish with watercress. Pour gravy into a separate bowl and serve with pork. Makes 6 to 8 servings.

Citrus pork marinade. In a bowl, mix 1 cup **dry white wine**, 2 teaspoons grated **orange peel**, 1 teaspoon grated **lemon peel**, and ¾ cup **orange juice**. Stir in 2 cloves **garlic** (minced or pressed), 1 **bay leaf**, and ¼ teaspoon **pepper**.

Pork-citrus gravy. Skim and discard fat from **pan drippings**. Add remaining **marinade** to drippings. Scrape bottom of pan to loosen brown bits; transfer liquid to a wide frying pan.

Set frying pan over medium heat and stir in 1 can (14½ oz.)

beef or chicken broth and ½ cup whipping cream. Bring to a boil and cook, stirring, until reduced to about 2 cups. Combine 1 tablespoon cornstarch with 2 tablespoons water and stir until smooth; add to gravy mixture. Cook, stirring, until gravy boils and thickens. Season with salt to taste.

SHERRIED PORK CHOPS & PEARS

Winter pears bake alongside these spicy chops. Rice pilaf and buttered Brussels sprouts make excellent accompaniments.

6	center-cut pork chops, each about ¾-inch thick
	Salt
3	firm-ripe Anjou pears
2	tablespoons lemon juice
¼	cup firmly packed brown sugar
½	teaspoon ground cinnamon
¼	cup dry sherry
1	tablespoon firm butter or margarine, divided into six equal pieces
½	teaspoon cornstarch mixed with 1 teaspoon water

Trim a little fat from chops and place fat in a wide frying pan over medium heat. Stirring, heat fat until pan is lightly greased. Without crowding, add pork chops and brown well on all sides. Sprinkle chops lightly with salt and arrange in center of convection oven roasting pan (without rack).

Cut each pear in half lengthwise, core, and remove stem and blossom end. Arrange pears, cut sides up, around chops; sprinkle meat and fruit with lemon juice. In a small bowl, stir together brown sugar and cinnamon, then sprinkle over meat and fruit; pour sherry over all. Put piece of butter in each

pear hollow. Bake, uncovered, in 325° convection oven for 40 to 45 minutes or until chops are tender and browned. Transfer chops and pears to a warm platter; keep warm.

Pour pan juices into a small pan. Stir cornstarch mixture and add to juices; cook, stirring, until sauce boils and thickens. Pour over pork and pears. Makes 6 servings.

OVEN-BARBECUED HERBED SPARERIBS

Traditional spareribs, crusty with a lively barbecue sauce, are irresistible when baked in a convection oven.

	4 to 5 pounds pork spareribs, cut in serving-size pieces
¾	cup bottled tomato-based chili sauce
½	cup apricot preserves
½	cup dry sherry or apple juice
¼	cup lemon juice
3	cloves garlic, minced or pressed
1½	tablespoons instant minced onion
1	teaspoon ground ginger
1½	teaspoons salt
1	teaspoon marjoram leaves
½	teaspoon each oregano leaves and pepper

Place spareribs in a single layer on rack over convection oven roasting pan. Bake, uncovered, in 400° convection oven for 45 minutes.

Meanwhile, in a small bowl, combine chili sauce, apricot preserves, sherry or apple juice, lemon juice, garlic, onion, ginger, salt, marjoram, oregano, and pepper. Remove ribs from oven; pour off and discard fat

from pan. Reduce convection oven temperature to 350°, then return ribs to oven and baste with about half of the chili sauce mixture. Bake, uncovered, turning and basting with remaining sauce, for 30 to 45 more minutes or until tender and glazed. Makes 4 to 6 servings.

LEG OF LAMB, ROSEMARY

Pictured on page 23

For a festive meal, consider this savory roast lamb with a rice pilaf or gratin of potatoes baked in the same convection oven.

1	clove garlic, minced or pressed
½	teaspoon ground ginger
¼	teaspoon each salt and pepper
	About 5-pound leg of lamb
1	large onion, unpeeled
1	sprig (about 6 inches) rosemary or ¾ teaspoon dry rosemary
1	can (14½ oz.) beef broth
1	tablespoon each cornstarch and water
2	tablespoons each catsup and soy sauce
½	teaspoon grated lemon peel

Combine garlic, ginger, salt, and pepper; rub over lamb. Place lamb, fat side up, on rack over convection oven roasting pan. Rinse onion and pierce a hole through it. Pull rosemary through hole or poke in dry rosemary; place onion near roast in pan.

Bake, uncovered, in 300° convection oven, basting often with broth, for 1¼ to 1½ hours (about 17 minutes per pound) or until a meat thermometer inserted in thickest portion registers 150° to 155° for medium. Remove lamb to a platter; cover lightly with foil and keep warm.

(Continued on page 25)

Convection cooking is at its best when turning out superbly browned, tender roasts like this leg of lamb with rosemary (recipe on facing page). Juices from the roast are the base for a savory gravy. Rice and wheat pilaf (recipe on page 54) makes an excellent accompaniment.

SLOW COOKING IN A CONVECTION OVEN

Slow oven-simmering transforms less tender cuts of meat into marvels of flavor and succulence. You can use your convection oven at a low-heat setting to work these wonders—just leave the meat to bake unattended for several hours. The best containers for this sort of cooking are enameled metal casseroles and Dutch ovens.

FLEMISH POT ROAST

Simmered in beer with lots of onions, this oven pot roast has an abundant golden sauce that is delicious with fluffy mashed potatoes.

- 3 tablespoons butter or margarine
  4-pound boneless beef chuck roast
- 4 medium-size onions, sliced
- 2 tablespoons flour
- 1 can or bottle (12 oz.) beer
- 1 tablespoon <u>each</u> brown sugar and red wine vinegar
- 1 bay leaf
- 2 cloves garlic, minced or pressed
- 1½ teaspoons salt
  Chopped parsley for garnish

In a 5 to 6-quart Dutch oven over medium-high heat, melt 1 tablespoon of the butter. Add roast and brown well on all sides. Spoon off fat. In a wide frying pan over medium heat, melt remaining 2 tablespoons butter; add onions and cook, stirring frequently, until pale golden. Sprinkle with flour and cook, stirring, until bubbly. Remove from heat and gradually stir in beer, then stir in brown sugar, vinegar, bay leaf, garlic, and salt. Return to heat and cook, stirring, until mixture begins to boil; then pour over meat.

Bake, covered, in 250° convection oven for about 5 hours or until meat is very tender when pierced. Remove meat to a warm serving dish; keep warm. Skim fat from cooking liquid, then cook, stirring, over direct heat (medium-high) until it boils and thickens slightly. Sprinkle meat with parsley, then slice. Spoon onion sauce over meat before serving. Makes about 8 servings.

OVEN-BAKED STROGANOFF

Round steak is the meat in this good-tasting dish. Serve it with buttered noodles.

- ¼ cup butter or margarine
- 2 pounds bottom round beef steak, cut in thin strips
- 1 large onion, thinly sliced
- ½ pound mushrooms, sliced
- 2 tablespoons flour
- 1 clove garlic, minced or pressed
- 1 teaspoon salt
- ¼ teaspoon pepper
- ¼ cup <u>each</u> dry red wine and tomato paste
- 1 bay leaf
- 1 cup beef broth
- ½ cup sour cream
  Chopped parsley for garnish

In a wide frying pan over medium heat, melt 2 tablespoons of the butter. Add beef strips, about half at a time, and brown on all sides. Transfer strips, as they brown, to a deep 3-quart baking pan. In the same frying pan, melt remaining 2 tablespoons butter; add onion and mushrooms and cook until golden. Remove pan from heat and mix in flour, garlic, salt, pepper, wine, tomato paste, bay leaf, and broth. Stir to blend, then pour mixture over meat.

Cover tightly and bake in 250° convection oven for about 4 hours or until meat is very tender when pierced. Remove from oven and mix in sour cream. Sprinkle with parsley. Makes 6 servings.

Skim fat from pan juices, discard onion. Pour juices through a wire strainer into a medium saucepan over medium heat. In a small bowl, stir together cornstarch and water; stir into juices along with catsup, soy sauce, and lemon peel. Cook, stirring, until sauce is thickened and clear. Pour into a separate bowl to be served with sliced lamb. Makes 6 to 8 servings.

GREEK PASTITSIO CASSEROLE

A splendid dish for a buffet, this rich casserole combines ground lamb in a savory sauce with macaroni and a custardlike topping.

- 1½ **pounds lean ground lamb**
- 2 **medium-size onions, chopped**
- 1 **clove garlic, minced or pressed**
- 1 **can (14½ oz.) Italian-style pear-shaped tomatoes**
- ½ **cup dry red wine**
- 2 **tablespoons each tomato-based chili sauce and chopped parsley**
- 1 **teaspoon each oregano leaves and salt**
- ¾ **teaspoon ground cinnamon**
- ¼ **teaspoon pepper**
- 2 **eggs**
- 8 **ounces elbow macaroni, cooked and drained**
- 2 **tablespoons butter or margarine, melted**
  Custard topping (recipe follows)
- 2 **cups (6 oz.) freshly shredded Parmesan cheese**

In a frying pan over medium heat, place lamb, onions, and garlic. Cook, stirring, until meat is lightly browned and onions are soft; drain off excess fat. Add tomatoes and their liquid (break up tomatoes with a spoon), wine, chili sauce, parsley, oregano, salt, cinnamon, and pepper. Cook, uncovered, stirring occasionally, for 10 minutes or until most of the juices have evaporated; remove from heat.

Meanwhile, separate eggs; set aside yolks for custard topping. Beat egg whites until slightly foamy and stir into lamb mixture; set aside. Toss macaroni with butter and set aside. Prepare custard topping and set aside.

To assemble casserole, spread half the macaroni in a greased shallow 3-quart baking pan; sprinkle with a third of the cheese. Distribute all the meat mixture over cheese, followed by remaining macaroni, and then another third of the cheese. Pour custard topping over cheese and spread evenly. Sprinkle with remaining cheese. If made ahead, cover and refrigerate.

Bake, uncovered, in 300° convection oven for 45 to 55 minutes (about 1 hour, if refrigerated) or until top is golden brown. Makes 8 to 10 servings.

Custard topping. In a 2-quart pan over medium heat, melt ¼ cup **butter** or margarine. Stir in ⅓ cup all-purpose **flour** and ¼ teaspoon each **salt**, ground **nutmeg**, and **white pepper**. Cook, stirring, until bubbly. Gradually stir in 2½ cups **milk** and cook, stirring constantly, until mixture boils and thickens; remove from heat. In a small bowl, beat together the 2 **reserved egg yolks** and 1 whole **egg**. Stir ¼ cup of the white sauce into eggs, then return egg mixture to sauce and stir until smooth.

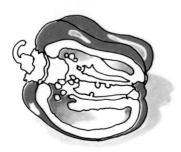

GREEK-STYLE LAMB SHANKS

Here is another carefree oven-simmered main dish—lamb shanks in a tomato sauce seasoned in the Greek manner. You can accompany it with zucchini-rice casserole (page 54).

- 4 **lamb shanks (¾ to 1 pound each)**
  Salt and pepper
  Flour
- 1 **large onion, thinly sliced**
- 1 **medium-size green pepper, seeded and cut in strips**
- 1 **can (8 oz.) tomato sauce**
- 1 **clove garlic, minced or pressed**
- ⅓ **cup dry white wine or chicken broth**
- ½ **teaspoon each salt and oregano leaves**
- ¼ **teaspoon each sugar, ground cinnamon, and dry rosemary**
- 1 **teaspoon grated lemon peel**
- 1 **tablespoon chopped parsley**
  Crumbled feta cheese (optional)

Sprinkle lamb shanks lightly with salt and pepper, coat lightly with flour, and arrange in a 4 to 5-quart Dutch oven or deep baking pan. Scatter onion and green pepper over top. In a medium-size bowl, combine tomato sauce, garlic, wine, salt, oregano, sugar, cinnamon, and rosemary; pour over meat. Bake, covered, in a 350° convection oven for 2½ to 3 hours or until lamb is browned and very tender when pierced.

Remove lamb shanks to a warm, rimmed serving platter; keep warm. Skim fat from cooking liquid, then stir liquid and pour over lamb. Garnish with lemon peel and parsley; sprinkle with cheese, if desired. Makes 4 servings.

A cluster of fresh bay laurel proclaims this golden roast chicken a winner. And your guests will proclaim you <u>chef extraordinaire</u> when you serve chicken laurel flamed with orange liqueur and accompanied by peas and orange slices. The recipe is on page 28.

26

Poultry

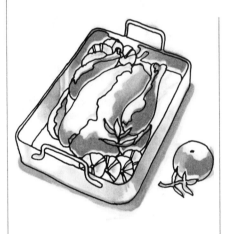

Crackling crisp skin the color of burnished gold concealing a tender, juicy interior—that's the way a perfectly roasted chicken, turkey, or any other bird should look and taste. Convection cooking is at its best delivering just such picture-perfect, juicy roast poultry.

Though there are several ways to determine if a whole roast bird is done—from jiggling a drumstick to slashing the meat—the most reliable test is to use a meat thermometer. Inserted into the thickest part of the thigh, the thermometer will register 180° to 185° F (170° to 180° F for turkey) when the bird is done. Cover the bird lightly with foil and let it stand for several minutes as you prepare gravy or finish side dishes. The standing time distributes the juices and settles the meat for carving.

In addition to roasting whole poultry superbly and in accelerated time, convection cooking also does a good job of oven frying chicken, as well as baking casseroles and chicken or turkey pies.

Adapting your own recipes.
Most standard oven roasting charts for poultry recommend 375° F for roast chicken and 325° F for roast turkey. Lower the temperature 25° for convection roasting; no preheating is necessary. For times and internal temperatures, check the chart for roasting poultry on page 29.

Recipes calling for chicken pieces coated in a batter and baked are easy to adapt for convection cooking. Just lower the temperature of your favorite recipe by 25° (usually from 375° to 350° F) and bake for the time suggested; 10 to 15 minutes before the time is up, check for overbrowning and test for doneness. The same formula applies when you're adapting recipes for any uncovered casserole-type dish or pie: lower the temperature 25° and watch for overbrowning. Covered poultry dishes can be convection cooked without changing time or temperature.

ROAST CHICKEN À LA PROVENÇALE

For a very hearty roast chicken, try filling it with a rice and chard stuffing and then serving it with a piquant tomato sauce.

4 to 5-pound roasting chicken
1 **bunch (about 1 lb.) Swiss chard**
¼ **cup olive oil or salad oil**
¼ **cup pine nuts**
1 **medium-size onion, chopped**
1 **clove garlic, minced or pressed**
¾ **cup cooked brown or white rice**
¼ **cup grated Parmesan cheese**
1 **teaspoon dry rosemary**
Salt and pepper
Provençale tomato sauce (recipe follows)

Remove giblets from chicken; reserve liver and set remaining giblets aside for other uses. Rinse chard and drain well. Remove white stem from each leaf. Cut stems into ¼-inch slices and coarsely chop leaves; set aside in separate piles.

Heat oil in a wide frying pan over medium heat. Add nuts and cook, stirring, until golden. Remove nuts and set aside. Stir in onion, chard stems, and garlic. Cover and cook for 4 to 5

minutes or until chard stems are fork-tender. Add chicken liver, if desired, and cook until no longer pink when slashed. Stir in chard leaves, cover, and cook for about 3 minutes or until leaves are wilted. Remove from heat and mix in nuts, rice, cheese, and rosemary. Add salt and pepper to taste.

Rinse chicken and pat dry. Stuff neck and body cavities with chard mixture and secure skin over openings with small skewers.

Place chicken, breast down, on rack over convection oven roasting pan. Roast, uncovered, in 350° convection oven for 30 minutes. Turn chicken, breast up, and continue roasting for 1 more hour (allow 16 to 20 minutes per pound in all) or until chicken is golden brown and meat near thigh bone is no longer pink when slashed.

Meanwhile, prepare Provençale tomato sauce.

Transfer chicken to a platter. Serve meat and stuffing with Provençale tomato sauce. Makes 6 servings.

Provençale tomato sauce. Heat ¼ cup **olive oil** or salad oil in a 3-quart pan over medium heat. Add 1 large **onion** (chopped) and cook until the onion is soft. Add 1 can (15 oz.) **Italian-style tomatoes** (broken up with a spoon) and their liquid, ¼ cup each **dry white wine** and **chicken broth**, 1 clove **garlic** (minced or pressed), ¾ teaspoon each crushed **fennel seed** and dry **rosemary**, 1 strip of **orange peel**, 1 **bay leaf**, and ½ teaspoon **sugar**. Bring to a boil. Cover, reduce heat, and simmer for 20 minutes; then uncover and continue simmering for about 25 more minutes or until most of the liquid has evaporated. Remove bay leaf and orange peel. Add **salt** and **pepper** to taste. Stir in 12 to 16 pitted **ripe olives.** If made ahead, cool, cover, and refrigerate; reheat just before serving.

CHICKEN LAUREL

Pictured on page 26

When you have guests for dinner, here's a handsome presentation: plump roast chicken adorned with a cluster of fresh bay (laurel) leaves and flamed with orange liqueur. Orange slices and peas accompany the bird.

4½ to 5-pound roasting chicken
Salt
½ **large, unpeeled orange, cut in chunks**
½ **medium-size onion, sliced**
2 **or 3 bay leaves**
About 2 tablespoons butter or margarine
¼ **teaspoon grated orange peel**
⅓ **cup orange juice**
2 **or 3 cups hot cooked peas, drained**
1 **or 2 large oranges, peeled, white membrane removed, and sliced**
Small cluster fresh bay leaves (or 3 or 4 dry bay leaves)
3 **tablespoons orange-flavored liqueur**

Remove giblets from chicken; reserve for other uses. Rinse chicken and pat dry. Lightly sprinkle chicken inside and out with salt. Fill neck and body cavities with orange chunks, onion slices, and the 2 or 3 bay leaves. Secure skin over body cavities with skewers.

Place chicken, breast up, on rack over convection oven roasting pan. Roast chicken, uncovered, in 350° convection oven for about 1½ hours (16 to 20 minutes per pound) or until chicken is golden brown and meat near thigh bone is no longer pink when slashed. After 30 minutes, rub chicken with a little of the butter to moisten skin. Rub with butter one or two

ROASTING POULTRY

Kind of poultry	Convection roast temperature (Fahrenheit)	Minutes per pound	Internal temperature when done (Fahrenheit)
CHICKEN			
Broiler-fryer, whole, 2–3½ pounds	350°	16–20	180°–185°
Broiler-fryer, quartered, 3–3½ pounds	350°	13–18	—
Broiler-fryer, parts, 3–3½ pounds	350°	13–18	—
Roasting, whole, unstuffed, 3½–5 pounds	350°	16–20	180°–185°
CORNISH HEN			
Unstuffed, ¾–1½ pounds	350°–375°	16–20	180°–185°
Stuffed, ¾–1½ pounds	350°	18–23	180°–185°
TURKEY			
Whole, unstuffed, 10–16 pounds	300°	14–19	170°–180°
Whole, unstuffed, 18–25 pounds	300°	11–15	170°–180°
Breast, half, 2½–3 pounds	300°	25–30	170°–180°

more times during roasting, using about 1 tablespoon in all.

Protecting your hands with pot holders, tip chicken to drain juices from body into roasting pan; transfer chicken to a platter and keep warm.

Skim off and discard fat from juices in roasting pan. Add orange peel and orange juice to pan; bring to a boil over medium heat and stir, scraping browned particles free from pan. Remove from heat; stir in remaining tablespoon butter until melted, then pour juices into a serving bowl.

Spoon hot peas around chicken and garnish with orange slices and the cluster of bay leaves.

Gently heat liqueur in a small pan over low heat until barely warm; set aflame and pour over chicken. Carve and serve, passing juices to spoon over each portion. Makes 6 servings.

ROAST CHICKEN WITH HERBS

For this savory, herb-speckled bird, you can use an economical, whole-body frying chicken. You can modify the seasonings by reducing the amount of garlic and herbs or by adding a little lemon juice to the herb-butter baste.

  3 to 3½-pound broiler-fryer chicken
  3 cloves garlic
  1 bay leaf
  3 tablespoons butter or margarine, melted
  ¾ teaspoon salt
  ½ teaspoon pepper
  ¼ teaspoon <u>each</u> dry thyme, sage, oregano, marjoram and basil

Remove giblets from chicken; set aside for other uses. Rinse chicken and pat dry. Split one clove of garlic and rub skin of chicken with cut sides of garlic.

(Continued on next page)

In chicken cavity place garlic (including cut clove) and bay leaf. Stir together butter, salt, pepper, thyme, sage, oregano, marjoram, and basil. Put about 1 tablespoon of the mixture into cavity of chicken. Generously brush chicken with remaining butter mixture.

Place chicken, breast up, on rack over convection oven roasting pan; tuck wing tips under chicken. Roast, uncovered, in 350° convection oven for about 1 hour (16 to 20 minutes per pound) or until chicken is golden brown and meat near thigh bone is no longer pink when slashed. Serve hot or cold. Makes 4 or 5 servings.

ROAST CHICKEN GOLDEN GATE

Here is another fine feast for a small dinner party. The chicken and its savory sauce are flavored with herbs and bacon.

4 to 5-pound roasting chicken

1	teaspoon salt
4	tablespoons butter or margarine, softened
1	clove garlic, minced or pressed
¼	teaspoon each ground ginger and white pepper
1	teaspoon fines herbes (or ½ teaspoon each dry rosemary and marjoram leaves)
2	teaspoons lemon juice
3	strips bacon
¼	pound mushrooms, chopped
1	tablespoon finely chopped onion
3	tablespoons dry sherry
½	cup water

Remove giblets from chicken; reserve liver and set remaining giblets aside for other uses. Rinse chicken and pat dry. Sprinkle salt inside cavity. Mix 2 tablespoons of the butter with garlic, ginger, pepper, fines herbes, and lemon juice. Rub on outside of chicken.

Place chicken, breast up, on rack over convection oven roasting pan; tuck wing tips under chicken. Roast, uncovered, in 350° convection oven for 1 hour. Cut bacon strips in halves and place across breast and legs. Continue roasting for about 30 more minutes (allow 16 to 20 minutes per pound in all) or until chicken is golden brown and meat near thigh bone is no longer pink when slashed. Transfer to a platter and keep warm.

Meanwhile, in a small pan over medium heat, melt remaining 2 tablespoons butter. Add mushrooms, onion, and chicken liver; cook until liver is lightly browned. Remove liver, mash with a fork, and return to mushroom mixture. Add sherry, bring to a boil, and cook until most of the liquid is gone; remove from heat. When chicken is done, spoon off and discard fat from pan drippings. Add water to drippings and scrape browned particles free from pan. Add to mushroom mixture and stir until blended. Bring to a boil over medium heat, then pour into a serving bowl and serve with carved chicken. Makes 6 servings.

PEKING-STYLE CHICKEN

In this simplified version of Peking duck, each guest receives a small chicken half, deftly seasoned and crisply roasted. Guests then remove pieces of chicken and roll them in warm flour tortillas spread with Chinese plum or hoisin sauce, slivered green onions, and sprigs of fresh coriander. Stir-fried zucchini makes a good side dish.

2	small broiler-fryer chickens (about 2½ lbs. each), cut in half lengthwise
4	quarts water
¼	teaspoon pepper
½	teaspoon each ground cinnamon and ginger
1	tablespoon each brown sugar and vinegar
2	teaspoons soy sauce
2	packages small flour tortillas (about 8 inches in diameter)
2	bunches green onions, cut into 2-inch-long slivers
	Hoisin or Chinese plum sauce
	Sprigs of fresh coriander (cilantro or Chinese parsley)

Rinse chicken halves. In a large kettle bring water to a boil. Remove from heat and immediately plunge chicken halves into water. Let stand for 1 minute; remove from water and pat dry.

In a small bowl, combine pepper, cinnamon, ginger, brown sugar, vinegar, and soy sauce. Brush all sides of chicken with mixture. Place chicken halves in a bowl; cover and refrigerate for 4 to 8 hours.

Lift chicken halves from bowl and place, skin side up, on rack over convection oven roasting pan. Bake, uncovered, in 400° convection oven for 40 to 45 minutes or until skin is richly browned and crisp and meat near thigh bone is no longer pink when slashed.

Meanwhile, unwrap tortillas and rewrap each stack in foil. Place in convection oven 15 minutes before chickens are done. Remove one stack and wrap in a napkin to serve. Keep second pack in warm convection oven with heat at a low setting until needed.

Serve chicken and tortillas, and pass small dishes of green onions, hoisin or plum sauce, and coriander sprigs. Makes 4 servings.

Chicken breasts Mexican style (recipe on page 32) celebrates a fiesta of Mexican flavors—avocado, lime, tomatoes, plus a crunchy cumin-and-chili-spiced coating that's baked on the chicken. It's delicious with Cheddar cheese popovers (recipe on page 73). Top the chicken with sour cream and pass the salsa!

CHICKEN BREASTS, MEXICAN-STYLE

Pictured on page 31

These colorful, well-seasoned chicken breasts are served nestled in a bed of shredded lettuce with tomatoes, avocado, and sour cream.

2 eggs
   Bottled green chile salsa or taco sauce
¼ teaspoon salt
1 cup fine dry bread crumbs
1 teaspoon each chili powder and ground cumin
¾ teaspoon garlic salt
¼ teaspoon oregano leaves
3 whole chicken breasts (about 1 lb. each), split, boned, and skinned
¼ cup butter or margarine
1 ripe avocado
4 to 6 cups shredded iceberg lettuce
   About 1 cup sour cream
4 green onions (including tops), thinly sliced
   12 to 18 cherry tomatoes
1 lime, cut in wedges

In a shallow bowl, beat together eggs, 3 tablespoons of the salsa, and salt. In another shallow bowl, combine bread crumbs, chili powder, cumin, garlic salt, and oregano. Dip each chicken piece into egg mixture and roll in crumb mixture, then dip into egg mixture and roll in crumb mixture again.

In a shallow baking pan large enough to hold chicken pieces in a single layer, melt butter in 350° convection oven. Remove pan from oven and add chicken pieces, turning to coat with butter. Bake, skin side up and uncovered, in 350° convection oven for about 25 minutes or until meat in thickest part is no longer pink when slashed. Just before chicken completes cook-ing, halve avocado lengthwise, remove pit, peel and slice.

To serve, arrange chicken on a bed of shredded lettuce. Top each piece with a dollop of sour cream. Garnish with green onions, tomatoes, lime wedges, and avocado. Pass extra sour cream and salsa. Makes 6 servings.

LEMON CHICKEN

Served with rice and broccoli or asparagus spears, this tart-sweet chicken dish makes a simple, appealing meal for company or family.

6 to 8 pieces of broiler-fryer chicken (breasts, legs, thighs)
2 lemons
⅓ cup all-purpose flour
1½ teaspoons salt
½ teaspoon paprika
¼ cup salad oil or shortening
2 tablespoons brown sugar
½ cup chicken broth
2 sprigs fresh mint

Rinse chicken pieces and pat dry. Grate peel from 1 of the lemons and set peel aside. Cut grated lemon in half and squeeze juice over chicken pieces to coat chicken thoroughly. In a paper bag, combine flour, salt, and paprika. Shake bag to lightly coat chicken pieces with mixture.

Heat oil in a wide frying pan over medium heat. Add chicken pieces and cook slowly until browned. Remove and arrange, skin side up, in single layer in a shallow baking pan.

Sprinkle grated lemon peel and brown sugar over chicken. Thinly slice remaining lemon and cover chicken with slices. Pour in broth and place mint over chicken.

Bake, covered, in 350° convection oven for 35 to 40 minutes or until meat near thigh bone is no longer pink when slashed. Remove mint before serving. Makes 6 to 8 servings.

SPICY OVEN-FRIED CHICKEN

Rice pilaf and your favorite green vegetable make the perfect accompaniment for these chicken quarters coated with a curry-spiced butter.

3 to 3½-pound broiler-fryer chicken, quartered
½ teaspoon salt
6 tablespoons butter or margarine
2 teaspoons each curry powder and Worcestershire
1 teaspoon oregano leaves
½ teaspoon each dry mustard and garlic powder
¼ teaspon paprika
3 dashes liquid hot pepper seasoning
1 chicken bouillon cube or 1 teaspoon chicken stock base

Rinse chicken quarters and pat dry. Sprinkle with salt and arrange, skin side down, in a shallow, rimmed baking pan or convection oven roasting pan.

In a small pan over medium heat, melt butter. Stir in curry, Worcestershire, oregano, mustard, garlic powder, paprika, liquid hot pepper, and bouillon cube. Generously brush some of the mixture over chicken pieces. Bake, uncovered, in 350° convection oven for 20 minutes.

Turn chicken pieces, skin side up, and again brush generously with butter mixture. Continue baking for 20 to 25 more minutes or until chicken is golden brown and meat near thigh bone is no longer pink when slashed. Baste one or two more times with butter mixture, using it all by the time chicken is done. Arrange chicken on a warm platter and drizzle with the butter mixture from baking pan. Makes 4 servings.

CRUNCHY CHICKEN

Those who like baked chicken extra crisp will enjoy this flavorful coating made with cornmeal and Parmesan cheese, plus sesame seeds and wheat germ.

⅓ **cup yellow cornmeal**

¼ **cup grated Parmesan cheese**

2 **tablespoons <u>each</u> sesame seeds and toasted wheat germ**

2 **teaspoons <u>each</u> garlic powder and parsley flakes**

1½ **teaspoons thyme leaves**

1 **teaspoon dry sage leaves**

½ **teaspoon <u>each</u> salt and pepper**

2 **tablespoons <u>each</u> butter or margarine and salad oil**

2 **eggs**

1 **tablespoon milk**

3 to 3½-pound broiler-fryer chicken, cut into pieces

In a bowl, combine cornmeal, cheese, sesame seeds, wheat germ, garlic powder, parsley flakes, thyme, sage, salt, and pepper. Put butter and oil in a shallow rimmed baking pan in 350° convection oven just until butter melts. In a shallow dish, beat eggs and milk until blended.

Rinse chicken pieces and pat dry. Dip each piece into egg mixture; drain briefly, then dip in cornmeal mixture, turning to coat thoroughly. Place pieces in baking pan, turning to coat with butter mixture. Bake, skin side up and uncovered, in 350° convection oven for about 45 minutes or until chicken is golden brown and meat near thigh bone is no longer pink when slashed. Makes 4 or 5 servings.

EASY BAKED CHICKEN KIEV

Prepare these succulent, herb-butter stuffed chicken breasts in advance, then bake them just before serving time for an impressive dish.

4 **whole chicken breasts (12 oz. <u>each</u>), split, boned, and skinned**

½ **cup (¼ lb.) butter or margarine, softened**

1 **teaspoon oregano leaves**

1 **tablespoon chopped parsley**

4 **ounces jack cheese**

½ **cup <u>each</u> fine dry bread crumbs and grated Parmesan cheese**

½ **teaspoon garlic salt**

¼ **teaspoon white pepper**

With a mallet, pound chicken breasts between pieces of wax paper until each is about ¼ inch thick. Prepare herb butter in a small bowl by combining ¼ cup of the butter, ¼ teaspoon of the oregano, and parsley; set aside. Cut jack cheese into 8 strips, each about ½ inch thick and 1½ inches long. Prepare crumb mixture in a shallow pan by combining bread crumbs, Parmesan cheese, garlic salt, pepper, and remaining ¾ teaspoon oregano. In a small pan, melt remaining ¼ cup butter.

Spread each chicken piece with herb butter and top with a strip of cheese. Fold opposite sides in far enough to overlap and seal in butter and cheese.

Starting with one narrow end, roll up until a neat bundle is formed. Dip in melted butter, drain briefly, then roll in crumb mixture. Arrange, seam side down and without touching, in a 7 by 11-inch baking pan. Drizzle with any remaining melted butter. Cover and refrigerate for at least 4 hours or until next day.

Bake, uncovered, in 350° convection oven for about 30 minutes or until chicken is well browned and meat in thickest part is no longer pink when slashed. Makes 8 servings.

HONEY-GLAZED BAKED CHICKEN

A honey and orange-flavored butter lends a fruity taste and a crisp crust to this chicken entrée. For an attractive presentation, you can garnish it with orange slices.

3 to 3½-pound broiler-fryer chicken, cut into pieces

2 **tablespoons butter or margarine**

⅓ **cup honey**

1 **teaspoon <u>each</u> salt, dry mustard, and grated orange peel**

¾ **teaspoon garlic powder**

⅛ **teaspoon pepper**

Peeled orange slices, for garnish

Rinse chicken pieces and pat dry; arrange, skin side up, in a single layer in a shallow rimmed baking sheet. Bake, uncovered, in 400° convection oven for about 20 minutes or until chicken begins to brown.

Meanwhile, in a small pan over medium heat, melt butter. Add the honey, salt, mustard, orange peel, garlic powder, and pepper; stir until the ingredients are well blended. Reduce convection oven temperature to 350°. Generously brush chicken

A loaf of bread (crusty French), a jug of wine (dry white), two crisp-skinned Cornish hens (convection roasted, of course)—oh, yes—and thou! Here's a simple but romantic supper for two, worthy of Omar Khayyám. The recipe for herb cheese Cornish hens starts on the facing page.

pieces with all the honey-butter mixture. Return pan to oven and continue baking, uncovered, for about 25 more minutes or until chicken is richly browned and meat near thigh bone is no longer pink when slashed.

Arrange chicken pieces on a platter. Drizzle with pan drippings, if desired. Garnish with orange slices. Makes 4 or 5 servings.

CHICKEN & ARTICHOKE CASSEROLE

For a complete convection oven meal, you might bake this chicken with the barley and pine nut casserole on page 55.

3 to 3½-pound broiler-fryer chicken, cut into pieces
Salt, pepper, and paprika
¼ **cup butter or margarine**
1 **can (14 oz.) artichoke hearts, drained and halved**
¼ **pound mushrooms, sliced**
2 **tablespoons all-purpose flour**
⅔ **cup chicken broth**
3 **tablespoons dry sherry**
¼ **teaspoon dry rosemary**

Rinse chicken pieces and pat dry. Lightly sprinkle each piece with salt, pepper, and paprika; set aside.

In a wide frying pan over medium heat, melt butter. Add chicken, a few pieces at a time, and cook until browned on all sides. Arrange chicken, skin side up, in a shallow 3-quart baking pan and tuck artichokes around pieces; set aside.

Discard all but 3 tablespoons of the pan drippings. Add mushrooms and cook until golden. Stir in flour and cook for 1 minute. Remove from heat and gradually mix in broth, sherry, and rosemary. Return to heat and cook,

stirring, until sauce boils and thickens. Pour over chicken and artichokes. Bake, covered, in 350° convection oven for 35 to 40 minutes or until meat near thigh bone is no longer pink when slashed. Makes 4 or 5 servings.

CHILE-CHEESE BAKED CHICKEN

Complement this hearty, Mexican-flavored chicken casserole with rice or refried beans and a green salad with orange slices.

3 to 3½-pound broiler-fryer chicken, cut into pieces
Flour
2 **tablespoons salad oil**
1 **can (15 oz.) tomato sauce**
½ **cup water**
2 **chicken bouillon cubes, crushed**
1 **can (4 oz.) diced green chiles, drained**
1 **can (4¼ oz.) chopped ripe olives, drained**
2 **tablespoons each instant minced onion and white wine vinegar**
¾ **teaspoon each ground cumin and garlic salt**
2 **cups (8 oz.) shredded Cheddar cheese**

Rinse chicken pieces and pat dry. Lightly coat with flour. Heat oil in a wide frying pan over medium heat; add chicken and brown on all sides. As pieces brown, arrange them, skin side up, in a shallow baking pan.

Pour off excess oil in frying pan and wipe pan clean. To pan, add tomato sauce, water, crushed bouillon cubes, chiles, olives, onion, vinegar, cumin, and garlic salt. Bring to a boil. Reduce heat and simmer, uncovered, for about 3 minutes or until sauce thickens slightly. Pour over chicken.

Bake, covered, in 350° con-

vection oven for 35 to 40 minutes or until meat near thigh bone is no longer pink when slashed. Remove from oven, skim off and discard fat, if necessary, and sprinkle chicken with cheese. Return to convection oven and bake, uncovered, for 5 to 8 more minutes or until cheese melts. Makes 4 or 5 servings.

BAKED CHUTNEY CHICKEN

The exotic flavor and rich brown glaze of this chicken might suggest tedious preparation, but it couldn't be simpler. Serve the chicken with hot fluffy rice and a tart fruit salad.

3½-pound broiler-fryer chicken, cut into pieces
⅓ **cup each soy sauce and Major Grey chutney**
Parsley sprigs

Rinse chicken pieces and pat dry. Place chicken in a bowl and pour soy sauce over pieces. Let stand for about 15 minutes, turning often.

Lift chicken pieces from bowl and arrange, skin side up, in single layer in a shallow rimmed baking sheet. Brush evenly with chutney (finely chop large pieces). Bake, uncovered, in 350° convection oven for 45 to 50 minutes or until meat near thigh bone is no longer pink when slashed. Arrange chicken on a platter; garnish with parsley. Makes 4 or 5 servings.

HERB CHEESE CORNISH HENS

Pictured on page 34 and cover

What's more perfect for a festive dinner for two than golden brown, cheese-flavored Cornish game hens? Serve with crusty French bread to dip into the melted cheese inside the hens.

(Continued on next page)

2 **Rock Cornish game hens (18 to 24 oz. <u>each</u>), thawed if frozen**

White pepper and ground nutmeg

1 **package (4 to 5 oz.) garlic and herb-flavored creamy appetizer cheese**

2 **tablespoons butter or margarine, melted**

Remove giblets from hens and set aside for other uses. Rinse hens and pat dry. Lightly sprinkle with pepper and nutmeg. Place half of cheese inside each hen. Tuck wings under.

Arrange hens, breast down, on rack over convection oven roasting pan. Brush with melted butter. Roast, uncovered, in 375° convection oven for 30 minutes. Turn hens, breasts up, brush with pan drippings, and continue roasting for 20 to 25 more minutes or until hens are well browned and legs move easily when jiggled. Makes 2 servings.

TURKEY-BACON LOGS

Lean ground turkey, shaped into fat little sticks or logs and swirled with bacon, makes a quick supper dish. Stir-fry your favorite combination of vegetables for a crisp accompaniment.

1 **egg**

¼ **cup fine dry bread crumbs**

¼ **teaspoon <u>each</u> salt and white pepper**

1 **pound ground turkey**

¼ **cup <u>each</u> minced parsley and chopped green onion (including tops)**

8 **strips bacon**

Beat egg in a bowl; mix in bread crumbs, salt, and pepper and let stand for about 1 minute. Add turkey, parsley, and green onion; mix lightly until blended. Divide

mixture into 8 equal portions and shape each into a 2-inch-long log. Wrap a strip of bacon around each log, and secure end of each strip with a wooden pick.

Place on rack over convection oven roasting pan. Bake logs, uncovered, in preheated 425° convection oven for 25 to 30 minutes or until bacon is browned and crisp. Makes 4 servings.

ROAST TURKEY BREAST

Here is a flavorsome way to roast a half turkey breast. You can slice it for dinner, or keep it on hand to use in sandwiches, casseroles, or salads.

2½ **to 3-pound half turkey breast, thawed if frozen**

3 **tablespoons butter or margarine, softened**

2 **tablespoons chopped parsley**

½ **teaspoon grated lemon peel**

¼ **teaspoon <u>each</u> thyme leaves and salt**

⅛ **teaspoon <u>each</u> ground sage and white pepper**

1 **small clove garlic, minced or pressed**

Place turkey breast, skin side down, on rack over convection oven roasting pan. Mix together butter, parsley, lemon peel, thyme, salt, sage, pepper, and garlic until well blended. Rub bony side of turkey breast with about a third of the butter mixture. Bake, uncovered, in 300° convection oven for 45 minutes. Turn, skin side up, and rub with another third of the seasoned butter, then return to 300° convection oven. Bake, uncovered, spooning over remaining butter mixture occasionally, until a meat thermometer inserted in thickest part registers 170° to

180° (allow 25 to 30 minutes per pound in all) and juices run clear when turkey is pierced in center. Let stand, lightly covered with foil, for 10 to 15 minutes before slicing. Makes 6 to 8 servings.

TURKEY LEGS WITH FIVE-SPICE

The elusive flavors of Chinese five-spice—a blend of anise, cinnamon, ginger, allspice, and cloves—perfume these tenderly baked drumsticks.

4 **turkey legs (<u>each</u> about 1¼ lbs.)**

1 **cup water**

¼ **cup soy sauce**

½ **cup thinly sliced green onions (including tops)**

1 **clove garlic, minced or pressed**

1½ **teaspoons Chinese five-spice (or ½ teaspoon <u>each</u> ground cinnamon and ginger, ¼ teaspoon <u>each</u> ground allspice and crushed anise seeds, and ⅛ teaspoon ground cloves)**

2 **tablespoons <u>each</u> cornstarch and water**

Place turkey legs in a glass baking dish or plastic bag. Stir together the 1 cup water, soy sauce, green onions, garlic, and five-spice. Pour over turkey, cover or seal, and refrigerate for 4 hours or until next day, turning several times.

Transfer turkey legs to a baking pan just large enough to hold them in a single layer. Pour marinade over them. Bake, covered, in 325° convection oven for 45 minutes; turn legs and continue baking for another 45 minutes. Uncover and bake for 45 to 60 more minutes, turning once or twice, or until turkey is very tender when pierced. Remove legs from pan; arrange on a platter and keep warm.

Skim off and discard fat from pan juices; pour juices into a pan. Stir together cornstarch and water. Add to pan juices and cook, stirring, over medium heat until sauce boils and thickens. Pour sauce into a separate bowl or pour over turkey. Makes 4 servings.

ROAST TURKEY & YAMS WITH PORT CREAM GRAVY

You need not wait for the holidays to serve this delicious unstuffed roast turkey, richly glazed with cream and Port and baked with chunky yams.

> **12 to 13-pound turkey, thawed if frozen**
> **Salt and pepper**
> **Softened butter or salad oil**
> 4 **pounds large yams (5 or 6)**
> **Boiling salted water**
> ⅔ **cup each whipping cream and Port wine (or apple juice)**
> 1½ **tablespoons firmly packed brown sugar**
> **Chicken broth or water, if needed**
> ½ **cup all-purpose flour blended with ½ cup cold water**

Remove giblets from turkey; set aside for other uses. Rinse turkey and pat dry. Sprinkle cavities with salt and pepper. Rub turkey with butter. Pin neck skin to back of turkey with a skewer. Without trussing, arrange turkey, breast down, on rack over convection oven roasting pan. Roast turkey,

uncovered, in 300° convection oven for 1½ hours.

Meanwhile, wash and peel yams; cut crosswise into 2-inch-thick slices. Place in a pan of boiling salted water. After water returns to a boil, cook for 10 minutes; drain well and set aside.

In a bowl, prepare basting sauce by combining cream, Port, and brown sugar, then stir until sugar is dissolved. Set aside.

Remove turkey from convection oven. With hands protected, lift turkey and drain its juices into roasting pan; move rack and turkey to another pan. Scrape browned particles free from roasting pan and pour drippings into a large measuring cup; reserve for gravy.

Dip potato slices into basting sauce and arrange in roasting pan. Turn turkey, breast up, and place on rack over potatoes. Insert meat thermometer into thickest part of thigh. Baste turkey liberally with sauce.

Return turkey to convection oven and continue roasting, basting bird frequently, until drumstick moves easily when jiggled and meat thermometer registers 170° to 180° (about 3 hours in all).

Place turkey on a platter. With a slotted spoon remove yams and arrange around turkey or place in a serving dish. Lightly cover both with foil to keep warm for 15 minutes before slicing.

To make the gravy, scrape remaining drippings and browned particles free from roasting pan and add to reserved drippings in cup. Skim off and discard most of the fat from drippings. If necessary, add broth or water to drippings to make 3½ cups. Pour into a 2-quart pan. Stir in flour mixture and cook, stirring, over medium heat until gravy boils and thickens. Add salt and pepper to taste. Pour gravy into a separate bowl to be served with turkey and yams. Makes 8 to 12 servings.

HONEY GLAZED ROAST DUCKLING

Those who prize the crisp golden skin of perfectly roasted duckling will enjoy this delicious curry and mustard-accented interpretation. For easy serving, cut the roast duckling into quarters with poultry shears or sturdy kitchen scissors.

> **4 to 5-pound duckling, thawed if frozen**
> 1 **small tart apple, unpeeled, cored, and cut into wedges**
> ½ **small onion, cut into wedges**
> 1 **teaspoon butter**
> 2 **tablespoons honey**
> 1 **tablespoon Dijon mustard**
> ¼ **teaspoon each salt and curry powder**

Remove giblets from duckling; reserve for other uses. Rinse duckling, pat dry, and remove excess fat. Place apple and onion wedges in cavity. Tie legs and tail together, skewer neck skin to back, tuck wings under, and pierce skin with a fork.

Place duckling, breast down, on rack over convection oven roasting pan. Roast, uncovered, in 350° convection oven for about 1¼ hours. Meanwhile, in a small pan over low heat, gently warm butter, honey, mustard, salt, and curry powder. Turn duckling, breast up, and brush with honey mixture. Continue roasting for 30 to 45 more minutes or until duckling is well browned and tender when pierced. Discard apple and onion. Cut duckling into quarters to serve. Makes 2 to 4 servings.

Seafood

Bacon-stuffed trout, crunchy oven-fried fish fillets, baked red snapper with piquant fresh tomato sauce—these are just a few of the seafood recipes that your convection oven can cook to perfection.

We're pleased to report that convection cooking is particularly well suited to baking fish. The seafood we tested came out exceptionally moist and tender.

Besides the simple baked fish dishes, you can enjoy convection-cooked seafood casseroles, oven-poached whole fish, and oven-fried, batter-coated fillets or oysters.

Adapting your own recipes. Any covered seafood dish can bake at about the same time and temperature given in your favorite recipe. Preheating the oven is not necessary.

Recipes that call for liquid of some kind and require cooking in an uncovered container, such as a gratin dish, can be very simply adapted for convection cooking—just lower the temperature 25° and bake for the same length of time specified in your recipe. Again, no preheating is necessary. Do check for overbrowning during the last few minutes, and test for doneness.

For recipes that require baking at high temperatures without liquid, you can reduce the temperature 25° to 50° (usually to 400° F); but preheat the oven first. Batter-coated seafood is often baked at high temperatures, too. We found that 400° to 425° F in a convection oven crisps the coating and cooks the seafood in about the same time as indicated in standard recipes calling for temperatures of 450° to 500° F.

Convection broiling requires preheating—usually to around 450° F. Seafood can be broiled on a baking sheet, and firm-fleshed fish steaks and whole fish can be convection broiled like meat, directly on the convection roasting rack. Brush the fish with butter or oil so it won't dry out. Convection broiling takes 2 or 3 minutes longer than broiling near the direct source of heat, but fish broiled on the rack needn't be turned.

Polka-dotted with sliced pimento-stuffed green olives, Veracruz-style red snapper features a whole fish baked the Mexican way—in a piquant fresh tomato sauce. The recipe is on page 44.

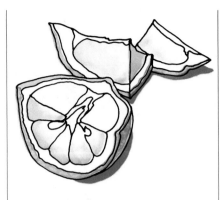

BACON-STUFFED TROUT

A savory bacon stuffing and a crunchy crumb-and-cheese coating give a wonderful flavor to this easy, oven-fried trout entrée.

4   strips bacon
1   medium-size onion, chopped
4   trout (about 8 oz. <u>each</u>)
2   bay leaves, split lengthwise
½   cup crushed seasoned croutons
¼   cup grated Parmesan cheese
⅛   teaspoon <u>each</u> garlic powder and white pepper
1   egg, beaten with 1 teaspoon water
¼   cup butter or margarine
    Lemon wedges

In a large frying pan over medium heat, cook bacon until crisp. Remove bacon from pan; drain and crumble. Discard all but 2 tablespoons drippings. Add onion and cook, stirring, until soft; stir in bacon.

Wipe trout with damp cloth, inside cavities and outside. Place 2 tablespoons of the bacon-onion mixture in cavity of each trout; top with half a bay leaf. Close cavity and secure with a skewer.

In a shallow pan, combine crushed croutons, cheese, garlic powder, and pepper. Dip trout in egg mixture; then roll in crouton mixture to coat.

Add butter to a shallow, rimmed baking sheet; set in convection oven while it preheats to 400°. Lay trout in pan and turn to coat with melted butter. Bake, uncovered, for 12 to 15 minutes or until fish flakes readily when prodded in thickest portion with a fork. Garnish with lemon. Makes 4 servings.

SALMON WELLINGTON

Baked in a puffy, golden pastry, salmon fillets make a distinguished dinner entrée that can be prepared in advance. The tangy lemon sauce, based on a reduction of the liquid in which the salmon was poached, can also be made ahead and reheated over hot (not boiling) water.

1½   pounds salmon fillet, about 1 inch thick
2   cups water
1   cup dry white wine
1   small carrot, thinly sliced
1   small onion, thinly sliced
1   bay leaf
10   whole black peppers
4   whole allspice
½   teaspoon <u>each</u> salt and thyme leaves
3   sprigs parsley
    Mushroom filling (recipe follows)
1   package (10 oz.) frozen patty shells, thawed
    Lemon sauce (recipe follows)

Wipe salmon with damp cloth. Cut salmon into 6 pieces, each about 3 inches square. In a wide frying pan over medium heat, combine water, wine, carrot, onion, bay leaf, black peppers, allspice, salt, thyme, and parsley. Cover and simmer for 15 minutes. Place salmon squares, skin side down, in liquid. Cover, reduce heat, and gently simmer just until salmon is almost light pink throughout (7 to 10 minutes). With a slotted spoon lift salmon from pan; discard skin. Cool, cover, and refrigerate. Reserve poaching liquid.

Prepare mushroom filling. On a floured board, roll out each patty shell to make an 8-inch circle. Spoon about 1 tablespoon of the mushroom filling in center of each circle of dough and top with a salmon square. Fold dough over salmon, overlapping edges; moisten edges to seal. Place pastry-wrapped salmon, sealed side down, on an ungreased rimmed baking sheet. If made ahead, cover and refrigerate.

Bake, uncovered, in a preheated 425° convection oven for 15 to 20 minutes or until pastry is golden brown. Serve with lemon sauce. Makes 6 servings.

Mushroom filling. In a frying pan over medium heat, melt 1 tablespoon **butter** or margarine. Add ½ pound **mushrooms** (sliced), and 2 **green onions** (thinly sliced). Cook, stirring, until liquid evaporates (5 to 10 minutes). Cool, cover, and refrigerate.

Lemon sauce. Strain reserved salmon poaching liquid (discard vegetables) into a pan and, if necessary, boil over high heat to reduce (or add water to increase) to 1½ cups. Stir together 1 tablespoon **each** cornstarch and **water**; add to poaching liquid and cook, stirring, until sauce boils and thickens.

Beat 3 **egg yolks** with 2 tablespoons **lemon juice**. Blend some of the hot sauce into the yolk mixture, then return all to pan. Reduce heat to very low and cook, stirring constantly, just until sauce thickens. Mix in 1 tablespoon drained **capers.** Cover and refrigerate. To reheat, place in top of a double boiler over hot (not boiling) water; stir often. Makes about 1½ cups.

SPINACH-STUFFED SOLE

You'll appreciate the qualities of this dish—it's easy to prepare, festive, and delicious. Serve the fish with sautéed mushrooms, buttered carrots, and a tomato and butter lettuce salad.

- 1 package (12 oz.) frozen spinach soufflé
- 6 sole fillets (about 1½ lbs. total)
  White pepper and nutmeg
- 1 can (10¾ oz.) condensed cream of mushroom soup
- 1 tablespoon dry sherry or lemon juice
- 1½ cups (6 oz.) shredded Swiss cheese

Let the soufflé stand at room temperature for 30 minutes, then cut into 6 equal-sized pieces.

Wipe sole fillets with damp cloth. Lightly sprinkle each fillet with pepper and nutmeg. Place a portion of soufflé on each fillet and wrap fish around it. Place fish bundles, seam side down, in a greased, shallow 2-quart baking pan.

In a bowl, stir together soup, sherry, and a dash each of white pepper and nutmeg; pour mixture over fish bundles. Sprinkle with cheese.

Bake, uncovered, in 350° convection oven for 30 to 35 minutes or until fish flakes readily when prodded in thickest portion with a fork. Makes 6 servings.

COMPANY FISH CASSEROLE

A puffed golden topping crowning dill-seasoned fillets of sole makes this a handsome dish for a special dinner.

- 1½ pounds sole fillets
- 1 teaspoon dill weed
- ½ teaspoon salt
- 1 tablespoon chopped parsley
- ½ cup dry white wine
  About ⅓ cup milk
- 3 tablespoons each butter or margarine and all-purpose flour
- 5 eggs, separated
- 3 tablespoons freshly grated Parmesan cheese

Wipe fish fillets with damp cloth. Arrange fish in a greased shallow 2½ to 3-quart baking pan. Sprinkle with dill, salt, and parsley; pour in wine.

Bake, covered, in 400° convection oven for 10 minutes. Leaving fish in pan, spoon cooking liquid into measuring cup. Add milk to make 1 cup liquid. In a pan over medium heat, melt butter. Blend in flour and cook, stirring, until bubbly. Gradually stir in liquid and continue cooking and stirring until sauce boils and thickens. Remove from heat and beat in egg yolks, one at a time. (If made ahead, cover, and refrigerate fish and sauce; discard excess liquid from fish before baking.)

Beat egg whites until soft peaks form; fold into sauce. Sprinkle 1 tablespoon of the cheese over fish, then cover with sauce. Sprinkle with remaining cheese.

Bake, uncovered, in 400° convection oven for 12 to 15 minutes (20 minutes, if refrigerated) until puffed and golden. Serve immediately. Makes 4 to 6 servings.

PARSEE FISH

This Pakistani-inspired fish recipe features the unusual combination of coconut, chiles, and cucumber. Served with steamed rice and tender-crisp broccoli spears, this is elegant enough for company.

- 4 large sole fillets (about 1½ lbs. total)
- 1 tablespoon flaked coconut
- 1 clove garlic
- 2 canned whole green chiles, seeded
- ½ teaspoon sugar
- 1 teaspoon salt
- 5 tablespoons milk
- 2 eggs
- ½ medium-size cucumber, peeled, seeded, and finely chopped
- 1 tablespoon butter or margarine
  Paprika

Wipe fish fillets with damp cloth. Arrange fish in a single layer in a greased shallow rimmed baking pan. In blender or food processor, combine coconut, garlic, chiles, sugar, salt, and 1 tablespoon of the milk; whirl or process until smooth. Spread mixture evenly over fish. Beat eggs and remaining 4 tablespoons milk; stir in cucumber and pour over fish. Dot with butter.

Bake, uncovered, in 350° convection oven for 20 to 25 minutes or until fish flakes readily when prodded in thickest portion with a fork. Arrange fish on warm plates; sprinkle with paprika. Makes 4 servings.

ALL-IN-ONE-OVEN MEALS

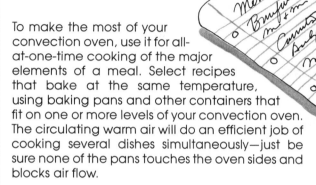

To make the most of your convection oven, use it for all-at-one-time cooking of the major elements of a meal. Select recipes that bake at the same temperature, using baking pans and other containers that fit on one or more levels of your convection oven. The circulating warm air will do an efficient job of cooking several dishes simultaneously—just be sure none of the pans touches the oven sides and blocks air flow.

Here are some suggested menus, made up—for the most part—of dishes for which recipes appear in this book.

* * *

Beef Roast in Brioche (page 12)
Broccoli with Cheese Topping (page 48)
Buttered Carrots
Fresh Strawberries in Port

* * *

Grated Carrot Meat Loaf (page 17)
Green Beans in Swiss Cheese Sauce (page 48)
Baked Potatoes   Green Salad
Crunch-top Rhubarb Pudding (page 94)

* * *

Ham Loaf with Sweet & Sour Glaze (page 20)
Sweet Potato Puff (page 51)
Peas with Sautéed Mushrooms
Orange Sherbet with Melon Balls or
Apricot-coconut Bars (make ahead, page 91)

* * *

Leg of Lamb, Rosemary (page 22)
Potatoes Gratin (page 51)
Whole Green Beans
Nockerln in Lemon Sauce (page 93)

* * *

Greek-style Lamb Shanks
(page 25)
Green rice (page 53)
Mixed Green Salad
Lemon Cake Pie (page 89)

* * *

Barbecue-style Swiss Steak (page 16)
Noodles Cooked in Broth
Cabbage Slaw with Green Pepper
Streusel Ginger Cake (page 85)

* * *

Spicy Oven-fried Chicken (page 32)
Rice & Wheat Pilaf (page 54)
Brussels Sprouts
Honey Peach Cobbler (page 94)

* * *

Chicken & Artichoke Casserole (page 35)
Barley & Pine Nut Casserole (page 55)
Italian Green Beans
Shredded Apple Custard Pie (page 88)

* * *

Roast Chicken with Herbs (page 29)
Quick Baked Chard (page 49)
Carrot Cornbread (page 75)
Ice Cream and Crisp Ginger Thins
(make ahead, page 90)

* * *

Bacon-stuffed Trout (page 40)
Asparagus Spears
Pilaf-stuffed Tomatoes (page 53)
Chocolate Mousse

* * *

Savory Fish Bake (page 43)
Rice & Cheese-stuffed Peppers (page 53)
Mixed Green Salad
Pear Crisp with Cheese (page 94)

SAVORY FISH BAKE

You can use either fresh or frozen sole in this saucy casserole with carrots and onion. Brown rice pilaf and a crisp green salad are good accompaniments.

2   **pounds sole fillets or 2 packages (1 lb. each) frozen sole fillets**
1   **small onion, thinly sliced**
¾   **cup shredded carrot**
1   **can (10¾ oz.) condensed cream of celery soup**
2   **tablespoons dry white wine or milk**
1   **tablespoon lemon juice**
½   **teaspoon marjoram or thyme leaves**
¼   **teaspoon garlic powder**
¼   **cup grated Parmesan cheese**
  Ground nutmeg

Wipe fresh fish with damp cloth. Place fillets, overlapping thin edges, in a greased 9 by 13-inch baking pan. Or place blocks of frozen fish (do not thaw) slightly apart in a single layer in a 7 by 11-inch baking pan. Arrange onion slices over fish; sprinkle carrots over onions.

In a bowl, stir together soup, wine, lemon juice, marjoram, and garlic powder. Pour mixture over fish. Sprinkle with cheese and lightly dust with nutmeg.

Bake, uncovered, in 350° convection oven for 20 to 25 minutes for fresh fish, 40 to 50 minutes for frozen or until fish flakes readily when prodded in thickest portion with a fork. Makes 6 servings.

MALAYSIAN SPICED FISH

Curry-scented spices puréed with onions season a whole rockfish in this recipe from Malaysia. If your convection oven isn't large enough to accommodate the entire fish, have the fish dealer remove the head.

  Curry paste (recipe follows)
1   **whole rockfish (about 3 lbs.), such as red snapper or rock cod, cleaned and scaled**
  Salad oil
  About 6 cups shredded lettuce
  Lemon wedges
  Sprigs of fresh coriander (cilantro or Chinese parsley) or parsley

Prepare the curry paste. Wipe fish with damp cloth, inside cavity and outside. Cut several deep diagonal slashes along each side of fish. Place a convection oven roasting pan (without rack) in convection oven while it preheats to 400°. Spread curry paste inside fish cavity and on one side of the fish. Remove hot pan from oven and add oil (oil should be ⅛ inch deep). Lay fish in pan, curry paste side down, spread remaining paste on top, and drizzle with some of the oil in pan.

Bake, uncovered, in 400° convection oven until fish flakes readily when prodded in thickest portion with a fork. Allow 10 to 12 minutes for each inch of thickness (measure fish in thickest portion), 20 to 25 minutes in all for a 3-pound fish.

Line a large serving platter with lettuce. With 2 wide spatulas, transfer fish to platter. Garnish with lemon and coriander. To serve, cut fish to the bone; then, sliding a wide spatula between flesh and ribs, lift off each serving. Makes 4 servings.

Curry paste. In a blender or food processor, put 3 tablespoons **lemon juice,** 2 to 4 tablespoons diced canned **green chiles,** 1 small **onion** (cut in small chunks), 2 cloves **garlic,** 1½ teaspoons **each** salt and **ground cumin,** and ¾ teaspoon **ground tur-**meric; whirl or process until smooth. Heat 3 tablespoons **salad oil** in a heavy frying pan over low heat. Cook the curry paste, stirring occasionally, until it thickens and begins to brown (about 6 minutes). Stir in ⅛ teaspoon **caraway seeds** and 1 tablespoon chopped fresh **coriander.**

VEGETABLE-TOPPED FISH FILLETS

For a colorful, nutritious main dish, try this quick recipe using fillets of red snapper or lingcod.

2   **pounds red snapper or lingcod fillets, each 1 inch thick**
  Salt, pepper, and tarragon
  Salad oil
3   **tablespoons butter or margarine**
1   **medium-size onion, chopped**
¼   **pound mushrooms, sliced**
1   **medium-size tomato, seeded and chopped**
¼   **cup each dry white wine and tomato-based chili sauce**
⅓   **cup grated Parmesan cheese**
  Chopped parsley

Wipe fish with damp cloth; cut large fillets into serving-size pieces and pull out as many bones as possible. Lightly sprinkle with salt, pepper, and tarragon. Place fillets in a greased, shallow, rimmed baking pan and drizzle each with about ½ teaspoon oil. Bake in a preheated 400° convection oven for 8 to 10 minutes or until fish flakes readily when prodded in thickest portion with a fork. Remove from oven, leaving oven on; spoon off and discard juices.

Meanwhile, in a medium-size

frying pan over medium heat, melt butter. Add onion and mushrooms and cook until onion is soft. Remove from heat and stir in tomato, wine, and chili sauce. Spoon mixture evenly over fillets, then sprinkle with cheese. Return to oven and bake for 3 to 5 more minutes or until cheese begins to melt. Sprinkle with parsley. Makes 4 to 6 servings.

VERACRUZ-STYLE RED SNAPPER

Pictured on page 39

A piquant fresh tomato sauce characterizes this popular Mexican method of baking a whole fish. Keep the accompaniments simple—steamed rice and green beans set off this fish to advantage.

2	tablespoons olive oil or salad oil
1	large onion, chopped
2	cloves garlic, minced or pressed
4	teaspoons sugar
1	teaspoon salt
¼	teaspoon <u>each</u> ground cinnamon and cloves
5	cups (about 5 large) peeled and chopped tomatoes
1½	teaspoons <u>each</u> lemon juice and water
1	tablespoon cornstarch
	1 to 2 fresh or canned jalapeño peppers, seeded and finely chopped
2	tablespoons capers
1	whole red snapper (or other rockfish), 4½ to 5 pounds, cleaned and scaled, head removed (if desired)
⅓	cup thinly sliced pimento-stuffed green olives
3	tablespoons finely chopped fresh coriander (cilantro or Chinese parsley) or parsley
	Lime slices

Heat oil in a 12-inch frying pan over medium heat. Add onion and garlic and cook, stirring, until onion is soft. Stir in sugar, salt, cinnamon, cloves, and tomatoes. Raise heat to medium-high and continue cooking and stirring until sauce thickens (about 8 minutes).

Mix together lemon juice, water, and cornstarch; stir into tomato mixture. Continue cooking and stirring until sauce boils and clears; remove from heat. Add peppers and capers.

Wipe fish with damp cloth, inside cavity and outside. Place a 24-inch length of foil crosswise in a convection oven roasting pan. Lightly grease foil and pan. Place fish in pan and pour tomato sauce over fish.

Bake, uncovered, in a preheated 400° convection oven for 30 to 40 minutes or until fish flakes readily when prodded in thickest portion with a fork. During the last 15 minutes, baste frequently with sauce.

Spoon off and discard watery juices from sauce; then stir sauce to blend. Lift foil, fish, and clinging sauce out of pan and slide fish and sauce onto a serving platter; spoon remaining sauce in pan over fish. Garnish with olives, coriander, and lime slices. To serve, cut fish to the bone; then, sliding a wide spatula between flesh and ribs, lift off each serving. Makes 4 to 6 servings.

CRUNCHY FISH BAKE WITH MUSHROOMS

You can choose from several varieties of fish fillets or steaks for this crisply baked seafood entrée. To complete the meal, serve a green salad, rice pilaf, buttered carrots, and a light refreshing dessert of orange or pineapple sherbet.

1½	pounds fish fillets (such as rockfish or lingcod), cut into serving-size pieces, <u>or</u> 1½ pounds fish steaks (such as halibut or swordfish)
	Salt and pepper
2	tablespoons lemon juice
6	ounces round buttery crackers or Cheddar cheese crackers, crushed to make 1½ cups fine crumbs
½	cup mayonnaise
2	tablespoons butter or margarine
6	ounces mushrooms, thinly sliced
⅓	cup thinly sliced green onions (including tops)
2	tablespoons chopped parsley
⅛	teaspoon thyme leaves
	Lemon wedges

Wipe fish with damp cloth. Sprinkle both sides with salt and pepper and drizzle with lemon juice. In a bowl, combine cracker crumbs and mayonnaise. Pat crumb mixture on both sides of fish and arrange in a single layer in a greased convection oven roasting pan (without rack) or shallow, rimmed baking pan. If made ahead, cover and refrigerate for up to 24 hours.

Bake, uncovered, in a preheated 425° convection oven for 12 to 18 minutes or until fish flakes readily when prodded in thickest portion with a fork and crumbs are lightly browned.

Meanwhile, in a medium-size frying pan over medium heat, melt butter. Add mushrooms and green onions and cook, stirring, until mushrooms are lightly browned. Stir in parsley, thyme, and salt and pepper to taste. Spoon mixture over fish. Garnish with lemon. Makes 4 servings.

SESAME OR ALMOND BAKED FISH

A dusting of sesame seeds or sliced almonds enhances almost any baked fish. You can use just about any favorite; red snapper, butterfish, flounder, sole, lingcod, and sea bass are among the many possibilities.

1½ pounds fish fillets or steaks, each ½ to ¾ inch thick
   Paprika
   All-purpose flour
2 tablespoons each butter or margarine and salad oil
¼ cup sesame seeds or sliced almonds
   Salt and pepper
   Lemon wedges

Wipe fish with damp cloth. Put a shallow, rimmed baking pan large enough to hold fish in a single layer in convection oven while it preheats to 425°. Lightly sprinkle fish with paprika, then coat with flour; shake off excess.

Remove pan from oven. Add butter and oil to pan and swirl until butter melts (fat should be about ⅛ inch deep). Lay fish in pan and turn to coat with melted butter. Sprinkle evenly with sesame seeds or almonds.

Bake, uncovered, in convection oven for 10 to 12 minutes or until fish flakes readily when prodded in thickest portion with a fork. Season with salt and pepper to taste. Garnish with lemon. Makes 4 to 6 servings.

BAKED HALIBUT & RICE

Halibut steaks or fillets bake atop a bed of custardy, dill-seasoned rice and vegetables. You need serve nothing more elaborate with this colorful dish than crusty bread and a green salad.

¼ cup (4 tablespoons) butter or margarine
1 medium-size onion, chopped
1 cup each thinly sliced celery and thinly sliced carrots
3 cups cooked rice (hot or cold)
¼ cup chopped parsley
½ teaspoon each dill weed and thyme leaves
1 teaspoon salt
1¼ cups milk, scalded
3 eggs
   2 to 3 pounds halibut steaks or fillets, about ¾ inch thick
   Salt and white pepper

In a large frying pan over medium heat, melt 3 tablespoons of the butter. Add onion, celery, and carrots and cook until almost fork-tender (about 7 minutes). Add rice, 2 tablespoons of the parsley, dill, thyme, and salt; cook, stirring, until heated through. Spread rice mixture in a greased 9 by 13-inch baking pan. In a bowl, gradually beat hot milk into eggs, then pour evenly over rice mixture.

Wipe fish with damp cloth. Sprinkle fish lightly with salt and pepper and arrange on rice. Melt remaining 1 tablespoon butter and drizzle over fish.

Bake, uncovered, in 350° convection oven for 25 to 30 minutes or until rice browns lightly and fish flakes readily when prodded in thickest portion with a fork. Sprinkle with remaining parsley. Makes 6 to 8 servings.

FISHERMAN'S CASSEROLE

Tiny shrimp and delectable crab, folded into a smooth cheese sauce and resting on a bed of rice, make an appealing casserole that can be assembled ahead of time. When ready to serve, bake this feast for 30 minutes and set it before your guests with a flourish.

5 tablespoons butter or margarine
1 medium-size onion, chopped
½ cup each chopped green pepper and chopped celery
¼ pound mushrooms, sliced
⅓ cup all-purpose flour
½ teaspoon salt
⅛ teaspoon ground white pepper
2 cups milk
2 cups (8 oz.) shredded sharp Cheddar cheese
1 pound small cooked shrimp
½ pound cooked fresh or frozen crab (thaw crab if frozen)
2 cups cooked rice
   Paprika

In a wide frying pan over medium heat, melt butter. Add onion, green pepper, celery, and mushrooms and cook until onion is soft, about 5 minutes. Blend in flour, salt, and pepper and cook, stirring, until bubbly. Gradually stir in milk and continue cooking and stirring until sauce thickens. Add cheese and stir until cheese melts. Remove from heat; fold in shrimp and crab.

Spread rice in a greased 9-inch-square baking pan. Spoon seafood mixture over rice; sprinkle lightly with paprika. If made ahead, cool, cover, and refrigerate.

Bake, uncovered, in 350° convection oven for 20 to 25 minutes (about 30 minutes, if refrigerated) or until lightly browned and heated through. Makes 6 servings.

DEVILED CRAB HUNTINGTON

An abundance of fresh crab stars in this make-ahead casserole. You may bake it either in one large pan or in individual ramekins.

    Crumb topping (recipe follows)
¼ **cup (4 tablespoons) butter or margarine**
¼ **pound mushrooms, sliced**
¼ **cup diced green pepper or celery**
¼ **cup all-purpose flour**
¼ **teaspoon salt**
    Dash each of white pepper and allspice
1 **teaspoon Dijon mustard**
2 **cups milk**
2 **tablespoons lemon juice**
¼ **cup dry white wine or milk**
2 **eggs, lightly beaten**
½ **cup mayonnaise**
1 **cup cooked rice**
    ¾ to 1 pound cooked fresh or frozen crab, thawed
1 **tablespoon chopped parsley**

Prepare crumb topping. In a large frying pan over medium heat, melt butter. Add mushrooms and green pepper and cook until mushrooms are lightly browned, about 5 minutes. Blend in flour, salt, pepper, allspice, and mustard and cook, stirring, until bubbly. Remove from heat and gradually stir in milk; cook and stir until sauce thickens. Remove from heat; add lemon juice, wine, eggs, mayonnaise, rice, crab, and parsley and mix well. Spread mixture in a shallow 2-quart baking pan or 6 ramekins. Sprinkle with crumb topping.

Bake, uncovered, in 350° convection oven about 30 minutes for large baking pan, 20 minutes for ramekins, or until browned and bubbly. Makes 6 servings.

Crumb topping. Melt ¼ cup **butter** or margarine; mix in ¾ cup soft **bread crumbs** and ¼ cup grated **Parmesan cheese.**

OVEN-FRIED OYSTERS

Crisply baked oysters are a treat any time, but they're especially tasty served with fresh asparagus.

2 **jars (10 oz. each) small fresh Pacific oysters**
½ **cup (¼ lb.) butter or margarine**
¾ **cup baking mix (biscuit mix)**
3 **tablespoons yellow cornmeal**
½ **teaspoon each garlic salt and paprika**
¼ **teaspoon pepper**
2 **eggs, lightly beaten**
2 **tablespoons chopped parsley**
    Lemon wedges

Drain oysters, cut in half if large, and pat dry. Add butter to a shallow, rimmed baking pan or convection oven roasting pan (without rack); set in convection oven while it preheats to 400°. When butter melts, remove pan from oven.

In a shallow pan, combine baking mix, cornmeal, garlic salt, paprika, and pepper. Dip each oyster in eggs; roll in cornmeal mixture, then in melted butter to coat. Arrange oysters, side by side, in pan.

Bake, uncovered, in a preheated 400° convection oven for about 15 minutes or until crisp and lightly browned. Remove from oven, transfer to a serving platter, and sprinkle with parsley. Garnish with lemon. Makes 4 servings.

HOT TUNA SANDWICHES

These sandwiches can be assembled ahead, wrapped, and kept on hand in the refrigerator; then, for a quick lunch or supper, bake and serve them with a mug of soup.

⅓ **cup mayonnaise**
3 **tablespoons prepared hamburger relish or sweet pickle relish**
1 **tablespoon Dijon mustard**
¼ **teaspoon seasoned salt or garlic salt**
⅛ **teaspoon pepper**
1 **can (6½ oz.) chunk-style tuna, drained**
1 **cup shredded Cheddar cheese**
¼ **cup each chopped green pepper and chopped celery**
¼ **cup thinly sliced green onions (including tops)**
3 **tablespoons chopped pimento-stuffed green olives**
6 **onion or Kaiser-style rolls**

In a bowl, mix together mayonnaise, hamburger relish, mustard, salt, and pepper. Add tuna, cheese, green pepper, celery, green onions, and olives and stir until well mixed.

Split rolls in half. Spread equal amount of tuna mixture on bottom half of each roll. Cover with top half of roll. Wrap each sandwich in foil. If made ahead, refrigerate.

Bake wrapped rolls in 350° convection oven for about 20 minutes if at room temperature, 30 minutes if chilled, or until cheese melts and sandwiches are heated through. Makes 6 sandwiches.

Vegetables & Side Dishes

The baked vegetable casseroles and other side dishes in this chapter are tasty enough to steal the spotlight from many a main dish. The classic French vegetable casserole, ratatouille (page 48), as well as cheese-gilded, carrot-stuffed potatoes (page 51) and pear-filled squash (page 50), are scene stealers guaranteed to win rave reviews from even the most anti-vegetable food critic in your family.

You can delight guests and family alike with mushrooms au gratin (page 49)—an elegant accompaniment for roast beef. Pilaf-stuffed tomatoes (page 53) is another delicious side dish for roast beef. And you won't want to miss our make-ahead version of green rice (page 53) to go with fish or poultry.

If you're looking for meatless main-dish ideas, you could serve savory cracked-wheat vegetable pilaf (page 55), protein-packed Cheddar rice casserole (page 54), or colorful rice and cheese stuffed peppers (page 53).

Since convection ovens can be filled to capacity to bake several dishes at once, we've timed most of the vegetable recipes in this chapter to bake along with whatever main course you are convection cooking. Most of the recipes turn out superbly at any of a range of temperatures, so you can bake the same recipe at 300° along with a roast, or at 350° along with a main dish that takes a higher temperature. The recipe directions specify the range of temperatures and times appropriate for each dish.

Adapting your own recipes.
Temperatures for uncovered casseroles can be lowered 25° to 100° to bake with another star attraction you might be baking in your convection oven. If you lower the temperature by 25°, figure the same time as in your standard recipe; but add 10 to 15 minutes to the time recommended in your standard recipe if you lower the temperature 75°; and add 20 to 30 minutes to the time if you lower the temperature by 100°.

Covered casseroles can be baked at the same temperature and time as given in a standard recipe, or you can lower the temperature and increase the time as for uncovered casseroles.

Potatoes, yams, and sweet potatoes can be convection baked 50° to 75° below the temperature usually recommended for a standard oven. Convection bake potatoes at 350° to 375° for 40 to 50 minutes. Bake yams and sweet potatoes at 350° to 375° for 30 to 45 minutes. Winter squash, such as acorn, Hubbard, butternut, or banana squash, should bake at 350° for 40 to 50 minutes.

BROCCOLI WITH CHEESE TOPPING

A Swiss cheese topping accented with mustard melts into broccoli as it heats in your convection oven.

1 **bunch (about 1½ lbs.) broccoli**
   Boiling salted water
1 **cup (4 oz.) shredded Swiss cheese**
⅓ **cup mayonnaise**
2 **tablespoons grated onion**
¼ **teaspoon salt**
⅛ **teaspoon ground white pepper**
½ **teaspoon Dijon mustard**

Separate broccoli into spears. Remove and discard tough ends; peel stems, if desired. In a wide frying pan, add broccoli to boiling salted water. Bring to a boil a second time, then reduce heat and cook until broccoli is tender-crisp when pierced (about 5 minutes). Drain broccoli and arrange on a heat-proof platter or shallow baking pan you can bring to the table. If made ahead, let stand at room temperature for up to 1 hour.

In a small bowl, combine cheese, mayonnaise, onion, salt, pepper, and mustard. Spoon cheese mixture evenly over broccoli. Bake, uncovered, in 300° to 350° convection oven for 18 to 25 minutes, or until broccoli is heated through and cheese is melted and lightly browned. Serve immediately. Makes 4 to 6 servings.

RATATOUILLE

The classic vegetable casserole from the south of France is a colorful complement to roast or barbecued lamb, and it can be served hot or at room temperature. If you have any left for a second time around, spoon it into a shallow casserole, top it with shredded Swiss cheese, and bake it in a convection oven until the cheese is crusty and golden. This makes an excellent first course or a meatless entrée.

1 **small onion, chopped**
1 **clove garlic, minced or pressed**
1 **medium-size (about 1 lb.) eggplant, cut into 1-inch cubes**
2 **medium-size zucchini, cut into 1-inch slices**
1 **can (1 lb.) tomatoes, broken up with a spoon**
1 **teaspoon dry basil**
½ **teaspoon salt**
3 **tablespoons olive oil or salad oil**
   Salt
   Sliced tomatoes and parsley sprigs (optional)

In a 3-quart Dutch oven or deep baking pan, combine onion, garlic, eggplant, zucchini, tomatoes, basil, the ½ teaspoon salt, and oil. Bake, covered, in 350° convection oven for 2 to 2½ hours, stirring once or twice, until eggplant is very soft. Season with salt to taste. If made ahead, cool, cover, and refrigerate.

Serve hot or at room temperature. Garnish with tomatoes and parsley, if desired. Makes 4 to 6 servings.

GREEN BEANS IN SWISS CHEESE SAUCE

Here's everyone's favorite — a green bean casserole that can be assembled in advance and baked in a convection oven.

1½ **pounds green beans**
    Boiling salted water
¼   **cup butter or margarine**
¼   **cup chopped onion**
½   **pound mushrooms, sliced**
2   **tablespoons all-purpose flour**
1   **teaspoon salt**
⅛   **teaspoon each ground white pepper and thyme or marjoram leaves**
1   **cup milk**
1   **cup (4 oz.) shredded Swiss cheese**
¼   **cup dry sherry or additional milk**

Break off and discard ends of beans; cut beans into 2-inch lengths. In a large pan of boiling salted water, cook beans until just tender; drain immediately and set aside. In a wide frying pan over medium heat, melt butter. Add onion and mushrooms and cook until soft (about 5 minutes). Blend in flour, salt, pepper, and thyme; cook, stirring, until bubbly. Gradually pour in milk and continue cooking and stirring until sauce boils and thickens.

Remove from heat and blend in ½ cup of the cheese and the sherry. Stir in beans and spread in a shallow 1½-quart baking pan. Sprinkle with remaining ½ cup cheese. If made ahead, cover and refrigerate.

Bake, uncovered, in 300° to 350° convection oven for 35 to 45 minutes (45 to 55 minutes, if refrigerated), or until beans are heated through and cheese is melted and lightly browned. Makes 6 servings.

CARROT & CAULIFLOWER MEDLEY

Two favorite winter vegetables combine colorfully in a creamy dish. You can make it ahead of time, then pop it in the oven to bake along with chicken or fish.

About 8 large carrots, peeled
1 **large head cauliflower**
Boiling salted water
2 **tablespoons butter or margarine**
2 **tablespoons all-purpose flour**
½ **teaspoon Dijon mustard**
1 **cup chicken broth**
½ **cup whipping cream**
1¼ **cups (5 oz.) shredded Swiss cheese**
2 **green onions (including tops), sliced**

Cut carrots into ¼-inch-thick diagonal slices (you should have 4 cups). Break cauliflower into flowerets. Cook vegetables in a large pan of boiling salted water until just tender (about 5 minutes). Plunge into cold water; drain and set aside.

In a medium-size pan over medium heat, melt the butter. Blend in flour and mustard and cook, stirring, until bubbly. Gradually pour in broth and cream and continue cooking and stirring until sauce boils and thickens. Gradually add 1 cup of the cheese, stirring until melted.

Combine vegetables and sauce in a shallow 2-quart baking pan. Sprinkle with remaining ¼ cup cheese. If made ahead, cover and refrigerate.

Bake, uncovered, in 300° to 350° convection oven for 25 to 30 minutes (about 35 minutes, if refrigerated) or until heated through. Garnish with onions. Makes 8 servings.

QUICK BAKED CHARD

Simple to prepare and quick to bake, this chard dish can be slipped into the convection oven during the last 15 minutes of roasting a chicken.

1 **bunch (about 1 lb.) Swiss chard**
¼ **cup butter or margarine**
1 **large onion, thinly sliced**
¼ **cup crisply cooked, drained, and crumbled bacon, or imitation bacon bits**
Seasoned salt and pepper
2 **eggs**
¾ **cup (3 oz.) shredded jack or Swiss cheese**

Rinse chard well and pat dry. Cut white stems from leaves. Cut stems crosswise into ¼-inch slices; set aside. Cut leaves crosswise into 1-inch strips; set aside separately.

In a wide frying pan over medium heat, melt butter. Add chard stems and onion and cook until onion is soft. Stir in chard leaves; cover and cook just until leaves are limp (2 to 3 minutes). Stir in bacon and season to taste with seasoned salt and pepper. Turn into a shallow 1½-quart baking pan. If made ahead, cover and refrigerate for as long as 24 hours.

Beat eggs until blended; pour over chard and sprinkle evenly with cheese. Bake, uncovered, in a 300° to 350° convection oven for 12 to 15 minutes (15 to 20 minutes, if refrigerated) or until eggs are set to your liking. Makes 4 to 6 servings.

MUSHROOMS AU GRATIN

Few vegetables can rival fresh mushrooms as an elegant companion for roast beef or steak— especially when combined with sour cream and cheese. Prepared ahead, this mushroom dish can be heated in the convection oven while the roast is standing before carving.

2 **tablespoons butter or margarine**
1 **pound mushrooms, sliced ¼ inch thick**
⅓ **cup sour cream**
¼ **teaspoon salt**
Dash of pepper
1 **tablespoon all-purpose flour**
¼ **cup finely chopped parsley**
½ **cup shredded Swiss or mild Cheddar cheese**

In a wide frying pan, over medium-high heat, melt butter. Add mushrooms and cook, stirring, until lightly browned. Cover pan until mushrooms exude juices (about 2 minutes). Blend sour cream with salt, pepper, and flour until smooth; stir into mushrooms and cook, stirring, until blended and beginning to boil. Spread in a shallow 1 to 1½-quart baking pan. Sprinkle with parsley and cheese. If made ahead, cover and refrigerate.

Bake, uncovered, in 350° convection oven for 15 to 20 minutes (20 to 25 minutes, if refrigerated) or until mushrooms are heated through and cheese is melted. Makes about 4 servings.

GREEN & WHITE VEGETABLE CASSEROLE

This medley of spinach and artichokes makes a generous quantity. You might serve it for company with a lamb or pork roast, or serve it as a meatless entrée for a light supper.

- 2 packages (10 oz. each) frozen chopped spinach, thawed
- 1 jar (6 oz.) marinated artichoke hearts
- 2 tablespoons butter or margarine
- 1 medium-size onion, chopped
- ¼ teaspoon ground nutmeg
- ¾ teaspoon oregano leaves
- 1 can (10¾ oz.) condensed cream of celery soup
- 4 eggs, beaten
- ⅛ teaspoon pepper
- 1 large package (8 oz.) cream cheese, softened
- ½ cup each milk and grated Parmesan cheese

Squeeze all moisture from spinach; set aside. Drain artichokes, reserving 2 tablespoons of the marinade; chop artichokes.

In a wide frying pan over medium heat, melt butter with reserved artichoke marinade. Add onion and cook, stirring, until onion is soft. Stir in spinach, artichokes, nutmeg, oregano, soup, eggs, and pepper. Spoon mixture into a greased shallow 2-quart baking pan; smooth top. Beat together cream cheese, milk, and Parmesan cheese; spread evenly over spinach mixture.

Bake, uncovered, in 300° convection oven for 35 to 40 minutes or until center feels firm when lightly pressed. Let stand for about 5 minutes before cutting into squares to serve. Makes 6 to 8 servings.

BAKED ZUCCHINI WITH MUSHROOMS

These tender, custardlike, delicately flavored vegetable squares can be assembled several hours before baking.

- 2 tablespoons butter or margarine
- ½ pound mushrooms, sliced
- ½ teaspoon salt
- ⅛ teaspoon each garlic salt and ground white pepper
- ¼ teaspoon Italian seasoning or oregano leaves
- 4 medium-size (about 1 lb. total) zucchini
- ¼ cup soft bread crumbs
- 4 tablespoons grated Parmesan or Romano cheese
- 4 eggs

In a wide frying pan over medium-high heat, melt butter. Add mushrooms and cook until most of the liquid has evaporated (about 5 minutes). Stir in salt, garlic salt, pepper, and Italian seasoning; set aside.

Finely shred zucchini. In a bowl, combine zucchini, bread crumbs, 2 tablespoons of the cheese, and mushroom mixture. Spoon into a greased 8-inch-square or shallow 2-quart baking pan. If made ahead, cover and let stand at room temperature for as long as 3 hours.

Beat eggs until blended, pour over zucchini mixture, and stir gently with a fork. Bake, uncovered, in 300° to 350° convection oven for 25 to 35 minutes or until custard is just set. Cut into squares and top with remaining 2 tablespoons cheese. Makes 6 to 8 servings.

PEAR-FILLED SQUASH

Slow-cooked onions and spiced pears make an appealing filling for acorn squash.

- ¼ cup butter or margarine
- 2 medium-size onions, sliced
- 2 pears, peeled, cored, and diced
- ½ teaspoon salt
- ¼ teaspoon each ground ginger and cinnamon
- 2 tablespoons dry sherry or apple juice
- 2 tablespoons brown sugar
- 3 small acorn squash, cut into halves and seeded
- ¼ cup sliced almonds

In a wide frying pan over low heat, melt butter. Add onions and cook, stirring as needed, until golden (about 30 minutes). Stir in pears, salt, ginger, cinnamon, sherry, and brown sugar. Increase heat to medium and cook for 2 minutes; remove from heat.

Arrange the squash, cut side down, in a greased shallow baking pan. Bake, uncovered, in 350° convection oven for 35 to 45 minutes or until almost tender when pierced. Turn the squash, cut side up, and mound pear mixture in each center; sprinkle with almonds. Bake for 10 to 12 more minutes or until squash is fork-tender and almonds are lightly browned. Makes 6 servings.

BUTTERY BAKED WINTER SQUASH

A touch of nutmeg turns plain baked winter squash into something special.

1½ to 2 pounds winter squash (banana or Hubbard); or 2 or 3 acorn or butternut, cut into halves

2 tablespoons butter or margarine

Salt, pepper, and ground nutmeg

Scrape away seeds and stringy portions of squash, if necessary. Arrange pieces or halves, cut side down, in greased shallow baking pan.

Bake, uncovered, in 350° convection oven for 35 to 40 minutes or until almost tender when pierced. Turn squash, cut side up, dot with butter, and sprinkle with salt, pepper, and nutmeg. Continue baking for 5 to 10 more minutes or until fork-tender and lightly browned. Makes 4 to 6 servings.

SWEET POTATO PUFF

Mashed banana adds natural sweetness to this simple casserole.

1 can (29 oz.) sweet potatoes or yams

1 large ripe banana

2 tablespoons butter or margarine, softened

2 eggs, separated

¼ teaspoon each ground nutmeg and ground ginger

6 large marshmallows

3 tablespoons sliced almonds

Drain sweet potatoes well. With an electric mixer, beat them

until smooth. Add banana, butter, egg yolks, nutmeg, and ginger; beat until smooth. In a bowl, beat egg whites until stiff peaks form; lightly fold beaten whites into sweet potato mixture. Spread in a well-greased shallow 1½ to 2-quart baking pan. At evenly spaced intervals, bury marshmallows in mixture; top with almonds.

Bake, uncovered, in 300° to 350° convection oven for 20 to 30 minutes or until sweet potatoes are heated through and almonds are lightly browned. Makes 6 servings.

CARROT-STUFFED POTATOES

Twice-baked potatoes, filled with a tangy yogurt, carrot, and bacon mixture and gilded with melted cheese, will be the star attraction at any meal.

4 medium-size russet potatoes

Butter or margarine

3 tablespoons milk

½ pint unflavored yogurt

2 tablespoons thinly sliced green onion (including top)

2 cups shredded carrots

4 strips bacon, crisply cooked, drained, and crumbled

Salt and pepper

1 cup (4 oz.) shredded sharp Cheddar cheese

Scrub potatoes well and pat dry. Rub skins with butter, then pierce with a fork. Bake in 350° convection oven for 40 to 50 minutes or until potato yields to gentle pressure.

Cut potatoes in half lengthwise. Scoop out pulp from each half, leaving about ¼-inch shell. Set shells aside. In a bowl, mash potato pulp until smooth, then beat in milk and yogurt until thoroughly combined. Stir

in green onion, carrots, bacon, and salt and pepper to taste. Mound potato mixture into shells and top evenly with cheese. Arrange stuffed halves in a shallow baking pan. If made ahead, cover and set aside for as long as 3 hours.

Bake, uncovered, in 350° convection oven for 15 to 20 minutes or until potatoes are heated through and cheese is melted and lightly browned. Makes 8 servings.

POTATOES GRATIN

Pictured on page 15

Baked with cream and a golden cheese crust, these potatoes are a French favorite with simply cooked meats such as lamb chops or steak.

2 pounds thin-skinned potatoes, peeled

Salt, ground white pepper, and ground nutmeg

1 cup whipping cream

¾ cup shredded Swiss or Gruyère cheese

Thinly slice potatoes (you should have 4 to 5 cups). Spread potatoes evenly in a greased shallow 1½-quart baking pan. Sprinkle lightly with salt, pepper, and nutmeg. Pour cream over potatoes.

Bake, uncovered, in 300° to 350° convection oven for 45 minutes to 1 hour or until potatoes are almost tender when pierced. Sprinkle with cheese and continue baking for 10 to 15 more minutes or until cheese melts and potatoes are browned. Makes 4 to 5 servings.

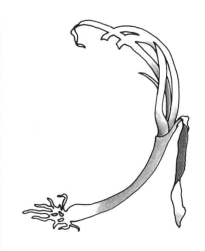

CHEESE-CARAWAY POTATOES

Everyone is so accustomed to mashed or sliced potatoes that cubed potatoes are a surprise. These well-seasoned potato cubes in a creamy, crumb-topped sauce are delicious with a meat loaf or roast.

- 3 large (about 1½ lbs.) thin-skinned potatoes, boiled and cooled
- 5 tablespoons butter or margarine, melted
- ⅓ cup thinly sliced green onions (including tops)
- 3 tablespoons all-purpose flour
- 1½ cups chicken broth
- 1 teaspoon caraway seeds
- ½ teaspoon ground cumin
  Salt and ground white pepper
- 1 cup (4 oz.) shredded Swiss cheese
- ½ cup soft bread crumbs
- ⅛ teaspoon paprika

Peel potatoes, if desired. Cut into ½-inch cubes and place in a shallow 1½-quart baking dish; set aside.

Place 3 tablespoons of the melted butter in a wide frying pan over medium heat. Add onions and cook until soft. Blend in flour and cook, stirring, until bubbly. Gradually stir in broth, caraway seeds, and cumin. Continue cooking and stirring until sauce boils and thickens. Add salt and pepper to taste.

Pour sauce over potatoes and top with cheese. Mix bread crumbs with paprika and the remaining 2 tablespoons melted butter; sprinkle over cheese. If made ahead, cool, cover, and refrigerate.

Bake, uncovered, in 300° to 350° convection oven for 25 to 35 minutes (35 to 40 minutes, if refrigerated) or until sauce is bubbly and crumbs are browned. Makes 4 to 6 servings.

POPULAR POTATO CASSEROLE

All the favorite garnishes for baked potatoes—bacon, green onions, sour cream, cheese, and crisp crumbs—embellish this irresistible potato casserole.

- 7 medium-size (about 2½ lbs.) thin-skinned potatoes
  Salted water
- 4 strips bacon, crisply cooked, drained, and crumbled
- 4 green onions (including tops), thinly sliced
- ⅓ cup milk
- ½ pint sour cream
- 1 cup (4 oz.) shredded Cheddar cheese
  Salt and pepper
- ¾ cup seasoned croutons, coarsely crushed
- 3 tablespoons butter or margarine, melted

Place potatoes in a 3-quart pan of boiling salted water. When water returns to a boil, cook, covered, until potatoes are just tender when pierced (about 20 minutes); drain well. When cool enough to handle, peel and cut into ¼-inch-thick slices.

In a greased shallow 2-quart casserole, arrange half the potato slices. Evenly distribute half the bacon and onions over potatoes. Stir milk into sour cream and spread half the mixture over onions; then cover with half the cheese. Season to taste with salt and pepper. Repeat layers. Sprinkle crouton crumbs over top and drizzle with butter.

Bake, uncovered, in 300° to 350° convection oven for 30 to 40 minutes or until heated through. Makes 6 servings.

CRUSTY POTATO CUPS

While the outside of each potato cup becomes browned and crusty, the inside remains creamy. You can serve the cups perched on tomato slices, with a dollop of sour cream on each.

- 3 medium-size (about 1½ lbs.) potatoes
- 1 medium-size onion, minced
- 1¼ cups (5 oz.) shredded Swiss cheese
- ½ teaspoon salt
- ¼ teaspoon each pepper and ground nutmeg
  Butter or margarine
  Paprika
  About 3 medium-size tomatoes, peeled, and cut into 12 thin slices (total)
  Sour cream

Peel potatoes. With a food processor or shredder, coarsely shred them. (If potatoes are not used immediately, place in a bowl of cold water to prevent discoloration; drain well and pat dry before using.) Mix potatoes with onion, cheese, salt, pepper, and nutmeg until well combined.

Generously butter 12 muffin

cups (about 2½-inch size); lightly sprinkle paprika over butter and press potato mixture evenly into each cup.

Bake, uncovered, in 350° convection oven for 40 to 50 minutes or until edges are well browned. Remove from oven and let cool for about 5 minutes. Loosen edges and invert each potato cup onto a tomato slice; spoon a dollop of sour cream onto each cup. Serve immediately. Pass additional sour cream to spoon over potatoes. Makes 6 servings.

PILAF-STUFFED TOMATOES

Fresh tomatoes make handsome, edible containers for well seasoned rice. Serve them with roast beef, lamb, or chicken.

- 2 tablespoons olive oil or salad oil
- 1 medium-size onion, chopped
- ½ cup rice
- 2 small cloves garlic, minced or pressed
- 1 cup chicken broth
- ¾ teaspoon salt
- ⅛ teaspoon pepper
- ½ teaspoon thyme leaves
- 6 medium-size firm tomatoes
- 2 tablespoons chopped parsley
- ⅓ cup grated Parmesan cheese

In a wide frying pan, heat 1 tablespoon of the oil over medium heat. Add onion and cook until soft and golden. Add rice and cook until lightly browned; stir in garlic. Add chicken broth, ½ teaspoon of the salt, pepper, and thyme. Cover, reduce heat, and simmer until liquid is absorbed and rice is tender (15 to 20 minutes).

Meanwhile, peel and core tomatoes. Cut a ½-inch-thick slice off core ends; set aside. With a spoon, scoop out seeds and pulp; discard seeds. Chop pulp and end slices. Sprinkle insides of tomato shells with remaining ¼ teaspoon salt; turn shells upside down to drain. Add chopped tomato and parsley to rice mixture. Place tomato shells in a shallow baking pan; fill shells with rice mixture.

Bake in 350° to 400° convection oven for 5 to 10 minutes or until rice is heated through. Remove tomatoes from oven and sprinkle them with cheese and remaining 1 tablespoon oil. Return to convection oven and bake for 6 to 8 more minutes or until cheese is lightly browned. Makes 6 servings.

RICE & CHEESE STUFFED PEPPERS

Curry-seasoned brown rice fills red or green peppers to make a festive vegetable dish.

- 3 large red bell or green peppers
  Boiling salted water
- 5 strips bacon
- 1 small onion, chopped
- 1 clove garlic, minced or pressed
- ¾ teaspoon curry powder
- 2 cups cooked brown rice
- 1 jar (2 oz.) sliced pimentos, drained
- 2 tablespoons chopped parsley
- 1½ cups (6 oz.) shredded Swiss cheese
- 1 egg, lightly beaten
  Salt and pepper

Cut each pepper in half lengthwise; remove and discard stem and seeds. Cook peppers, uncovered, in a large pan of boiling salted water for 2 minutes; drain.

In a wide frying pan over medium heat, cook bacon until crisp and well browned; drain, crumble, and set aside. Discard all but 1 tablespoon of the drippings. Add onion, garlic, and curry and cook until onion is soft. Remove from heat and stir in rice, pimentos, parsley, 1 cup of the cheese, egg, crumbled bacon, and salt and pepper to taste. Place drained pepper halves in a shallow 2-quart baking pan; fill halves with rice mixture. Sprinkle with remaining ½ cup cheese.

Bake, uncovered, in 300° to 350° convection oven for 20 to 30 minutes or until heated through. Makes 6 servings.

GREEN RICE

Always popular is the classic green rice casserole, with vegetables flavoring and coloring the rice. This make-ahead version flatters most meat, fish, and poultry entrées.

- 1 bunch (about 10 oz.) spinach
- 1 cup rice
- ¼ cup butter or margarine
- 2 teaspoons lemon juice
- ½ cup slivered or sliced almonds
- 1 clove garlic, minced or pressed
- 1 medium-size onion, chopped
- ½ teaspoon salt
- ½ cup each chopped green onions (including tops) and minced parsley
- 1 egg
- 1 cup milk

(Continued on next page)

Remove and discard stems from spinach. Wash leaves, drain well, and finely chop (you should have 2 cups, firmly packed); set aside.

In a large pan, cook rice according to package directions. Remove from heat; add butter, lemon juice, almonds, garlic, onion, salt, green onions, parsley, and spinach. Mix well.

Beat egg with milk; add to rice and mix lightly. Spread mixture in a greased 2½-quart baking pan. If made ahead, cover and refrigerate.

Bake, uncovered, in 300° to 350° convection oven for 30 to 45 minutes (45 minutes to 1 hour, if refrigerated) or until center is set. Makes 4 to 6 servings.

ZUCCHINI-RICE CASSEROLE

Zucchini, tomatoes, and two kinds of cheese join with rice in this brightly colored casserole.

2	tablespoons butter or margarine
1	medium-size onion, finely chopped
½	cup water
¼	teaspoon salt
3	or 4 medium-size (1 lb.) zucchini, sliced ¼ inch thick
½	green pepper, seeded and chopped
1½	cups cooked rice
1	can (8 oz.) tomato sauce
⅔	cup shredded jack, Swiss, or Cheddar cheese
¼	cup grated Parmesan cheese

In a small frying pan over medium heat, melt butter. Add onion and cook until soft; set aside. In a medium-size pan, combine water and salt and bring to a boil. Add zucchini and green pepper; cook, covered, until zucchini is almost tender (3 to 5 minutes). Drain well.

Gently combine onion, zucchini mixture, rice, and tomato sauce. Spread in a greased shallow 1½-quart baking pan. Mix together jack and Parmesan cheeses and sprinkle over top.

Bake, uncovered, in 300° to 350° convection oven for 15 to 20 minutes or until heated through. Makes 6 servings.

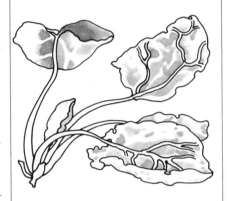

CHEDDAR RICE CASSEROLE

Chopped spinach adds color and flavor to this baked rice casserole with cheese.

1	cup rice
¼	cup butter or margarine
2	tablespoons chopped onion
1	package (10 oz.) frozen chopped spinach, thawed and well drained
1	tablespoon Worcestershire
½	teaspoon each marjoram and thyme leaves
4	eggs, lightly beaten
1	cup milk
2½	cups (10 oz.) shredded sharp Cheddar cheese Salt and pepper

Cook rice according to package directions. Meanwhile, in a small frying pan over medium heat, melt butter. Add onion and cook until soft. In a large bowl, combine rice, onion, spinach, Worcestershire, marjoram, thyme, eggs, milk, and 2 cups of the cheese. Season to taste with salt and pepper.

Spread mixture in a greased, shallow 2-quart baking pan and sprinkle with remaining ½ cup cheese.

Bake, uncovered, in 300° to 350° convection oven for 35 to 45 minutes, or until center is set. Makes 6 to 8 servings.

RICE & WHEAT PILAF

Pictured on page 23

Combining both quick-cooking brown rice and bulgur wheat, this flavorsome pilaf is a standout with unstuffed roast chicken or turkey.

¾	cup pine nuts or slivered almonds
½	cup (¼ lb.) butter or margarine
1	cup each quick-cooking brown rice and bulgur wheat
3½	cups chicken broth
1	teaspoon garlic salt
1	teaspoon Italian seasoning or thyme leaves
¾	cup minced parsley

Spread nuts in a shallow pan and toast in 350° convection oven, shaking pan occasionally, for 10 to 12 minutes or until nuts are lightly browned; set aside.

In a frying pan over medium-high heat, melt butter. Stir in rice and bulgur and cook, stirring, until rice begins to brown slightly. Add broth, garlic salt, and Italian seasoning; bring to a boil. Transfer mixture to a 2-quart baking pan.

Bake, covered, in 300° to 350° convection oven for 20 to 30 minutes or until liquid is absorbed. Remove from oven and stir in parsley and toasted nuts. Makes 6 to 8 servings.

CRACKED-WHEAT VEGETABLE PILAF

Made with nutlike bulgur wheat, this satisfying vegetable casserole can be served either as a meatless main dish or as a side dish with roast or broiled chicken.

Herbed tomato sauce (recipe follows)
1 cup bulgur wheat
1 cup chicken, beef, or vegetable broth (or water)
2 tablespoons chopped parsley
¼ cup diced green or red bell pepper or shredded carrot
½ cup thinly sliced green onions (including tops)
2 cups (about 8 oz.) finely diced Cheddar, Swiss, or jack cheese
1 cup whole kernel corn, cut off cob, or frozen and thawed
1 egg, lightly beaten

Prepare herbed tomato sauce.

In a bowl, combine bulgur and broth; let stand, stirring occasionally, until liquid is absorbed (about 1 hour). Stir in parsley, green pepper, onions, cheese, corn, and egg. Mix in tomato sauce. Spoon mixture into a greased shallow 1½-quart baking pan. If made ahead, cover and refrigerate.

Bake, covered, in 300° to 350° convection oven for 30 minutes. Uncover and bake for 10 to 20 more minutes until heated through. Makes 6 servings.

Herbed tomato sauce. In a bowl, mix together 1 can (8 oz.) **tomato sauce,** 1 teaspoon **dry basil,** ½ teaspoon **each oregano leaves** and **garlic salt,** and ¼ teaspoon **pepper.**

BARLEY & PINE NUT CASSEROLE

If you have used barley only in soup, you'll be pleasantly surprised by its appeal as a side dish, baked with pine nuts, onion, and herbs.

1 cup pearl barley
6 tablespoons butter or margarine
About ½ cup pine nuts or slivered almonds
1 medium-size onion, chopped
½ cup minced parsley
¼ cup minced chives or green onions (including tops)
¼ teaspoon each salt and pepper
2 cans (14 oz. each) beef or chicken broth
Parsley sprigs

Rinse barley with cold water; drain well. In a wide frying pan over medium heat, melt 2 tablespoons of the butter. Add pine nuts and cook, stirring, until lightly toasted. With a slotted spoon, remove nuts and set aside. To pan, add remaining 4 tablespoons butter, onion, and barley; cook, stirring, until lightly browned. Remove from heat and stir in pine nuts, parsley, chives, salt, and pepper. Spoon mixture into a 1½-quart

baking pan. If made ahead, cover and refrigerate.

In same frying pan, bring broth to a boil; then stir broth into barley mixture in baking pan. Bake, uncovered, in 300° to 350° convection oven for 1 to 1¼ hours or until barley is tender and liquid is absorbed. Garnish with parsley sprigs. Makes 4 to 6 servings.

SPICY BAKED LENTILS

Nourishing lentils are baked in a spicy tomato sauce to serve with barbecued steak, lamb, or pork. To make this casserole into a main dish, add frankfurters or smoked sausage links during the last 20 to 30 minutes in the convection oven.

1 package (12 oz.) lentils
1 teaspoon salt
About 3 cups water
4 strips bacon, finely diced
2 cans (8 oz. each) tomato sauce
1 medium-size onion, finely chopped
¼ cup firmly packed brown sugar
2 tablespoons prepared mustard
⅓ cup molasses

Rinse lentils well under cold water and discard any foreign material; drain thoroughly. Place lentils in a 2½ to 3-quart Dutch oven or deep baking pan. Add salt, 3 cups water, bacon, tomato sauce, onion, brown sugar, mustard, and molasses. Stir well.

Bake, covered, in 350° convection oven for about 2 hours or until lentils are soft and liquid is bubbly and thick. During baking, stir two or three times, adding a little more water if sauce becomes too thick. Makes 6 to 8 servings.

DEHYDRATING—DRYING FOODS THE CONVECTION WAY

If you can bear to give your convection oven a break from baking, you can use it to dehydrate your superabundant summer crops or irresistible seasonal buys of fruits, vegetables, and herbs.

Start with fresh, prime-for-eating produce. Then all you have to do is cut the food in uniform pieces. The thinner the pieces, the faster they'll dry.

Most vegetables require blanching to inactivate the enzymes that cause color and flavor deterioration. We prefer steam-blanching because it doesn't cause excessive loss of water-soluble nutrients.

Fruits that turn brown when exposed to air should be treated with an antioxidant, such as a commercial color keeper, or dipped in a mixture of two parts bottled lemon juice to one part water. Treating fruit with antioxidant helps it retain flavor and vitamin C.

Dehydration & storage. Foods dehydrate most effectively when the convection oven is set at 140° to 150° and the oven door is left ajar about half an inch. We suggest you rotate trays every few hours so that food dries evenly. Herbs dry quickly; you should check their progress after the first 45 minutes. Allow food to cool before testing them for dryness—dried vegetables should be leathery or brittle, fruits leathery and pliable; herbs should crumble easily when rubbed together.

Let dried foods cool completely before packaging them in airtight, moistureproof containers. Glass jars and plastic containers with tight-fitting lids work well; so does a plastic bag inside a plastic-lidded coffee can. Pack food as tightly as possible, but not so tightly that pieces get crushed. Herbs, in particular, retain their flavor longer if left whole.

Store the containers in a cool, dry, dark place—not a refrigerator, it contains too much moisture. Also, it's wise to label your containers. Identify the date on which you package the food, as well as the contents, because dehydrated food should not be kept longer than 6 to 10 months.

Rehydration. To rehydrate vegetables, soak them in liquid. Though different vegetables absorb different amounts of liquid, we recommend covering 1 cup dried vegetables with 1½ cups boiling water or broth and letting them stand for 20 to 30 minutes, stirring occasionally, until the vegetables have absorbed most of the liquid. If they absorb the liquid quickly but still look shriveled, add about ½ cup more boiling water and let stand until the shriveled look is gone. Cook rehydrated vegetables as you would fresh ones.

To rehydrate fruit, use room temperature tap water or fruit juice. As a general rule, cover 1 cup dried fruit with about 1½ cups liquid, and soak for 30 minutes to an hour. Since drying accentuates the natural sweetness of fruits, don't add sugar or a sweetening agent until rehydration is complete, and taste the fruit first to be sure it's necessary.

If you don't plan to use rehydrated foods within an hour after rehydration, cover and refrigerate them.

The dehydrating table that follows is a general guide. The length of time it takes to dehydrate foods varies, depending on the food's size and moisture content and the amount of food being dried at one time. Other variables include the humidity in the air and the oven temperature used.

FRUITS	Varieties best for drying	Preparation	Drying time in hours	Test for dryness
Apples*	Firm varieties: Gravenstein, Newtown Pippin, Rome Beauty, Winesap, and Jonathan	Peel, cut off both ends, core, and cut into ⅛-inch-thick slices	5–8	Soft, leathery, and pliable
Apricots*	Blenheim, Royal, and Tilton	Cut in half and remove pits	18–24	Soft, pliable, slightly moist in center when cut
Bananas*	Firm varieties	Peel, cut into ⅛-inch-thick slices	20–24	Leathery and pliable
Figs	Adriatic, Calimyrna, Mission, and Kadota	(Leave figs on tree; when fully ripe and ready for drying, they will fall to the ground.) Cut in half or leave whole	24–36	Leathery outside, but still pliable; slightly sticky inside, but not wet
Grapes	Thompson Seedless and Muscat	Leave whole; leave stems on until fruit is dried	16–24	Raisinlike and pliable
Nectarines and Peaches*	Freestone varieties	Cut in half and remove pits; peeling is optional but results in better-looking dried fruit	24–36	Soft, pliable, and slightly moist in center when cut
Pears*	Bartlett	Peel, cut in half, and core	24–36	Soft, pliable, slightly moist in center when cut
Persimmons	Firm varieties	Cut into ¼-inch-thick slices	8–24	Leathery
Pineapple		Cut off both ends; cut away rind and remove ''eyes''; cut into ¼-inch-thick rounds	16–20	Soft, pliable, and slightly moist in center when cut in half

*Fruits requiring an antioxidant (2 parts bottled lemon juice to 1 part water, or commercial antioxidant) applied to cut surfaces before drying, to prevent discoloration and loss of nutrients.

VEGETABLES

Carrots	Danvers Half Long, Imperator, Morse, Bunching, Nantes	Use only crisp, tender carrots. Cut off roots and tops. Peel, cut into ¼-inch-thick slices. Steam-blanch for 3 to 3½ minutes.	4–8	Tough to brittle
Mushrooms	Young, medium-size, with closed gills; hothouse varieties only—drying does not destroy toxins of poisonous varieties	Scrub, discard tough woody stems, and cut into ⅛-inch-thick slices. No blanching.	4–6	Very dry and leathery
Bell peppers	California Wonder, Merrimack Wonder, Oakview Wonder	Remove stem, seeds, and partitions. Cut into ½-inch-square pieces. No blanching.	3–6	Tough to brittle
Summer squash	Crookneck, Patty-pan, or Zucchini	Trim and cut into ⅛-inch-thick slices. Steam-blanch for 2½ to 3 minutes.	3–9	Brittle

HERBS & SPICES

Parsley and cilantro		Separate clusters; discard long or tough stems	1–3	Brittle and crumbly
Mint		Leave stems on until leaves are dried	1–3	Brittle and crumbly
Rosemary		(Cut stems when blossoms appear.) Leave stems on until leaves are dried.	1–3	Brittle and crumbly
Orange and lemon peel	Select rough-skinned fruit.	Use only zest (colored part of peel); if you include white part, peel will be bitter.	1–2	Tough to brittle

Note: Herbs dry very fast and require constant checking.

A sunburst of cheese-gilded tomato slices lets your guests know this is a quiche of a different flavor—cumin and caraway flavor, to be exact. The recipe for caraway cheese quiche is on page 61.

Eggs & Cheese

Lofty soufflés and puffy, crisp-crusted quiches are two of the best reasons for baking in a convection oven. Egg and cheese dishes bake higher and lighter in a convection oven because the warm swirling air maintains an even temperature, unlike the fluctuating temperature in most standard ovens.

Recipes like cheese-crusted mushroom soufflé (page 61), caraway cheese quiche (page 61), and ham and sour cream oven omelet (page 65) are just a few of this chapter's recipes that make magnificent brunch entrées. For a large group, you might consider serving the Mexican cheese puff (page 67)—it's a variation on the soufflé theme, yet holds its shape after cooking and makes 12 servings.

Egg and cheese treats such as soufflés and quiches are often associated with brunch or weekend breakfast, but look again—the recipes in this chap-ter also offer opportunities for savory late evening suppers, thrifty meatless meals, and make-ahead dinners. Custard cornmeal squares (page 65) make a delightful main dish served with fresh sliced tomatoes; and the baked mushroom frittata (page 67), filled with zucchini, salami, and mushrooms, is a meal in itself.

Adapting your own recipes. We had the best results baking soufflés and quiches at 350°—the same as (or slightly lower than) the temperature used for baking soufflés and quiches in a standard oven. Generally, we found that egg and cheese dishes baked in a convection oven at a temperature higher than 350° tended to get too brown on top. We also found that at 350°, convection ovens baked egg and cheese dishes from 5 to 10 minutes faster than the recommended time for the same kinds of recipes baked in a standard oven.

CLASSIC CHEESE SOUFFLÉ

A classic cheese soufflé is an economical way to impress guests or family. You can make it with a nippy Cheddar cheese or with a milder, more nutlike Swiss. To make a meal of the soufflé, you can also serve French bread, a simple lettuce salad, and chilled white wine.

3   tablespoons butter or margarine
    Dash of ground red pepper (cayenne)
½   teaspoon salt
¼   teaspoon dry mustard
3   tablespoons flour
1   cup milk
1   cup (4 oz.) shredded Cheddar or Swiss cheese
5   eggs, separated
    Butter or margarine

Preheat convection oven to 350°. In a 3-quart pan over medium heat, melt the 3 tablespoons butter. Add red pepper, salt, mustard, and flour and cook, stirring, until bubbly. Gradually pour in milk and continue cooking and stirring until sauce boils and thickens. Add cheese and stir until melted. Remove from heat and blend in egg yolks, one at a time, until well blended; set aside.

In a bowl, beat egg whites until short, moist peaks form. Fold half the beaten whites into egg yolk mixture; then carefully fold in remaining whites. Pour mixture into a buttered 7 to 8-cup soufflé dish. With tip of a spatula, draw a circle on surface of soufflé an inch or so in from rim of dish.

Bake in preheated 350° convection oven for 25 to 35 minutes, or until soufflé is golden brown and feels firm when lightly tapped. Serve immediately. Makes 3 or 4 servings.

CHEESE SOUFFLÉ WITH TARRAGON SHRIMP

A soaring cheese soufflé makes a spectacular main dish. Though it requires some effort, the results are well worth it.

Tomato-shrimp sauce
4   tablespoons butter or margarine
3   tablespoons finely chopped onion
1   small clove garlic, minced or pressed
2   medium-size tomatoes, peeled and diced
½   teaspoon salt
    Dash of ground white pepper
1   teaspoon dry tarragon
1   tablespoon chopped parsley
¼   cup dry white wine
1   pound medium-size raw shrimp, shelled and deveined
⅛   teaspoon ground red pepper (cayenne)
2   tablespoons brandy

Soufflé
3   tablespoons butter or margarine
3   tablespoons all-purpose flour
    Dash each of ground red pepper (cayenne), white pepper, and nutmeg
¼   teaspoon salt
1   cup milk
¼   cup shredded Parmesan cheese
1¼ cups (5 oz.) shredded Swiss cheese
5   eggs

To make shrimp sauce, melt 2 tablespoons of the butter in a frying pan over medium heat. Add onion and cook until soft. Mix in garlic, tomatoes, salt, pepper, and tarragon; continue cooking until tomatoes begin to soften (about 5 minutes). Add parsley and wine; reduce heat and simmer, uncovered, until sauce thickens (about 10 minutes).

Meanwhile, in a wide frying pan over medium heat, melt remaining 2 tablespoons butter. Add shrimp and cook, stirring, until they turn pink (about 45 seconds). Mix in red pepper and brandy. Add tomato sauce and remove from heat. Spread tomato-shrimp sauce in a well greased 7 to 8-cup soufflé dish.

To make soufflé, preheat convection oven to 350°. In a 3-quart pan over medium heat, melt butter. Blend in flour, red pepper, white pepper, nutmeg, and salt and cook, stirring, until bubbly. Gradually pour in milk and continue cooking and stirring until sauce boils and thickens. Add Parmesan cheese and 1 cup of the Swiss cheese; stir until melted, then remove from heat.

Separate eggs, blending egg yolks, one at a time, into sauce.

In a bowl, beat egg whites until short, moist peaks form. Fold half the beaten whites into egg yolk mixture; then carefully fold in remaining whites. Pour mixture over tomato-shrimp sauce in soufflé dish and sprinkle with remaining ¼ cup Swiss cheese. With tip of a spatula, draw a circle on surface of soufflé an inch or so in from rim of dish.

Bake in preheated 350° convection oven for 35 to 40 minutes or until soufflé is golden brown and feels firm when lightly tapped. Serve immediately, spooning some of the soufflé mixture and some of the shrimp sauce onto each plate. Makes 4 servings.

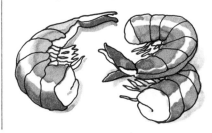

CHEESE-CRUSTED MUSHROOM SOUFFLÉ

Pictured on page 63

You can take a plain soufflé into more ambitious territory by incorporating buttery chopped mushrooms and green onion into it.

- 5 tablespoons butter or margarine
- ½ pound mushrooms, finely chopped
- 1 tablespoon chopped green onion (including top)
- ½ teaspoon salt
- ¼ teaspoon ground white pepper
  Dash of ground nutmeg
- 3 tablespoons all-purpose flour
- 1 cup milk
- 2 tablespoons dry sherry (optional)
- 1¼ cups (5 oz.) shredded Swiss cheese
- 5 eggs, separated
  Butter or margarine

Preheat convection oven to 350°. In a 3-quart pan over medium-high heat, melt the 5 tablespoons butter. Add mushrooms and onion and cook, stirring, until liquid has evaporated (about 5 minutes). Lower heat to medium; add salt, pepper, nutmeg, and flour and cook, stirring, until bubbly. Gradually pour in milk and sherry (if desired); continue cooking and stirring until sauce boils and thickens. Add 1 cup of the cheese and stir until melted. Remove from heat and blend in egg yolks, one at a time; set aside.

In a bowl, beat egg whites until short, moist peaks form. Fold half the beaten whites into mushroom mixture; then carefully fold in remaining whites. Pour mixture into a buttered 7-cup soufflé dish. Sprinkle top with remaining ¼ cup cheese. With tip of a spatula, draw a circle on surface of soufflé an inch or so in from rim of dish.

Bake in preheated 350° convection oven for 35 to 40 minutes or until soufflé is golden brown and feels firm when lightly tapped. Serve immediately. Makes 4 servings.

CHEDDAR SOUFFLÉ WITH PINEAPPLE

Crushed pineapple lends a unique, sweet flavor to this moist soufflé. Perfect for a luncheon or light supper, it should be served as soon as you remove it from the oven.

- 4 tablespoons butter or margarine
- ½ cup thinly sliced green onions (including tops)
- ¼ cup all-purpose flour
- ½ teaspoon salt
- ¼ teaspoon each ground white pepper and ground nutmeg
- 1 cup milk
- 1¼ cups (5 oz.) shredded sharp Cheddar cheese
- 4 eggs, separated
- 1 can (8 oz.) crushed pineapple, well drained

Preheat convection oven to 350°. In a 3-quart pan over medium heat, melt butter. Add onions and cook, stirring, for 1 minute. Blend in flour, salt, pepper, and nutmeg and cook, stirring, until bubbly. Gradually pour in milk and continue cooking and stirring until sauce boils and thickens. Add cheese and stir until melted. Remove from heat and blend in egg yolks, one at a time. Stir in pineapple.

In a bowl, beat egg whites until short, moist peaks form. Fold half the beaten whites into pineapple mixture; then carefully fold in remaining whites. Pour into a well greased 7 to 8-cup soufflé dish.

Bake in preheated 350° convection oven for 30 to 35 minutes or until soufflé is well browned and feels firm when lightly tapped. Serve immediately. Makes 4 to 6 servings.

CARAWAY CHEESE QUICHE

Pictured on page 58

Quiche—the French cheese-custard, first-course pie—enjoys popularity because of its versatility.

- Pastry for a single-crust 9-inch pie
  All-purpose flour
- 8 strips bacon
- 2 green onions (including tops), chopped
- 1½ cups (6 oz.) shredded kuminost (cumin and caraway-flavored) cheese
- 4 eggs
- 1¼ cups milk or half-and-half (light cream)
- 1 large, firm, ripe tomato
  Salt and pepper

Roll pastry out on a lightly floured board, then fit into a 9-inch pie pan. Flute edge. Bake in preheated 375° convection oven for 8 to 10 minutes or until crust begins to brown. Let cool on wire rack. Reduce convection oven temperature to 350°.

In a frying pan over medium heat, cook bacon until crisp;

drain, and crumble into partially baked pastry shell. Sprinkle with green onions and 1 cup of the cheese. In a bowl, beat eggs and milk; pour into pastry shell. Bake in preheated 350° convection oven for 30 to 35 minutes or until a knife inserted just off center comes out clean.

Meanwhile, peel tomato and cut into ¼-inch slices; cut each slice in half. Remove pie from convection oven and arrange tomato slices decoratively on top; lightly season with salt and pepper and sprinkle with remaining ½ cup cheese. Return to convection oven and bake for about 5 minutes or until cheese melts. Let stand for 5 minutes. Makes 4 to 6 servings.

LEEK & MUSHROOM QUICHE

For a simple dinner, serve this quiche favorite with fruit or a vegetable and crusty rolls.

    Pastry for a single-crust 9-inch pie
    All-purpose flour
½ pound mushrooms
4 tablespoons butter or margarine
1 cup thinly sliced leeks (white portion only)
1 cup (4 oz.) shredded Swiss or Gruyère cheese
3 eggs
1½ cups half-and-half (light cream)
½ teaspoon salt

Roll pastry out on a lightly floured board, then fit into a 9-inch pie pan. Flute edge. Bake in preheated 375° convection oven for 8 to 10 minutes or until crust begins to brown. Let cool on a wire rack. Reduce convection oven temperature to 350°.

Chop mushrooms but reserve 1 whole mushroom. In a large frying pan over medium heat, melt 2 tablespoons of the butter. Cook leeks until soft; transfer to a bowl. Add remaining 2 tablespoons butter to pan and cook chopped mushrooms until lightly browned and most of the liquid has evaporated; set aside.

Sprinkle ½ cup of the cheese into partially baked pastry shell. Cover evenly with leeks, then with mushrooms; sprinkle with remaining ½ cup cheese. In a bowl, beat eggs, half-and-half, and salt; pour into pastry shell. Slice reserved mushroom and arrange decoratively in center.

Bake in preheated 350° convection oven for 25 to 30 minutes or until a knife inserted just off center comes out clean. Let stand for 5 to 10 minutes. Makes 4 to 6 servings.

MUSHROOM CRUST QUICHE

A combination of sautéed mushrooms and crushed crackers forms the crust for this savory cheese and egg custard pie. Serve it with a fresh spinach or mixed green salad.

5 tablespoons butter or margarine
½ pound mushrooms, coarsely chopped
½ cup finely crushed saltine crackers
¾ cup chopped green onions (including tops)
2 cups (8 oz.) shredded jack or Swiss cheese
½ pint (1 cup) small or large-curd cottage cheese
3 eggs
⅛ teaspoon ground red pepper (cayenne)
¼ teaspoon paprika

In a frying pan over medium heat, melt 3 tablespoons of the butter. Add mushrooms and cook until soft. Stir in crushed crackers, then turn mixture into a well greased 9-inch pie pan. Press mixture evenly over bottom and up sides of pan.

In a frying pan over medium heat, melt remaining 2 tablespoons butter. Add onions and cook until soft. Spread onions over mushroom crust; sprinkle evenly with jack cheese. In a blender or food processor, whirl cottage cheese, eggs, and red pepper until smooth. Pour into crust and sprinkle with paprika.

Bake in 350° convection oven for 25 to 35 minutes or until a knife inserted just off center comes out clean. Let stand for 5 to 10 minutes before cutting. Makes 4 to 6 servings.

SHRIMP-OLIVE QUICHE

Cheese, shrimp, and sliced olives bake in this savory custard seasoned with mushroom soup. Serve it with slices of avocado and tomatoes.

    9-inch unbaked pastry shell, 1½ inches deep
2 cups (8 oz.) shredded jack cheese
½ pound small cooked shrimp
1 can (2¼ oz.) sliced ripe olives, drained
3 eggs
1 can (about 10¾ oz.) condensed cream of mushroom soup
¾ cup milk
¼ teaspoon each onion and garlic powder
    About 4 drops liquid hot pepper seasoning
    Paprika

Bake pastry shell in a preheated 375° oven for 8 to 10 minutes. Remove from oven and reduce oven temperature to 350°. Layer cheese, shrimp, and olives in pastry shell.

(Continued on page 64)

High, light, and handsome—that's how soufflés turn out in a convection oven. This soufflé contains buttery chopped mushrooms and Swiss cheese. Extra cheese sprinkled on top makes the crust especially tasty. You'll find the recipe for cheese-crusted mushroom soufflé on page 61.

Eggs & Cheese **63**

In a bowl, lightly beat eggs; stir in soup, milk, onion and garlic powders, and hot pepper seasoning. Pour over olives and sprinkle with paprika.

Bake in the preheated 350° oven for about 35 minutes or until a knife inserted just off center comes out clean. Let stand for 5 to 10 minutes before cutting. Makes 4 servings.

ITALIAN SAUSAGE & VEGETABLE QUICHE

You can make a nourishing family meal out of this meaty, substantial quiche.

	Pastry for a single-crust 10-inch pie
	All-purpose flour
10	ounces mild or hot Italian sausage
1	package (10 oz.) frozen Italian-style vegetables, thawed
¾	teaspoon garlic salt
1	teaspoon Italian seasoning or ¼ tsp. each dry basil and oregano, thyme and marjoram leaves
1½	cups (6 oz.) shredded sharp Cheddar cheese
4	eggs
1	cup half-and-half (light cream)

Roll pastry out on a lightly floured board, then fit into a 10-inch pie pan. Flute edge. Bake in preheated 375° convection oven for 8 to 10 minutes or until crust begins to brown. Let cool on a wire rack. Reduce convection oven temperature to 350°. Remove casings and crumble sausage into a frying pan over medium-high heat. Cook, stirring, until meat is browned. With a slotted spoon, lift out meat and reserve. Pour off and discard all but 1 tablespoon drip-

pings. Add vegetables, garlic salt, and Italian seasoning to drippings and cook, stirring, for 2 minutes; remove from heat. Stir in reserved sausage and cheese. Distribute evenly in partially baked pastry shell. In a bowl, beat eggs and half-and-half; pour over sausage-cheese mixture in shell.

Bake in preheated 350° convection oven for 25 to 35 minutes or until crust is browned and a knife inserted just off center comes out clean. Let stand for 5 to 10 minutes. Makes 6 servings.

MEXICAN CHORIZO & CHILE QUICHE

This piquantly flavored quiche is especially good with a cooling green salad that includes orange slices.

	Pastry for a single-crust 10-inch pie
	All-purpose flour
¾	pound chorizo sausage
¼	cup sliced green onions (including tops)
¼	cup bottled green taco sauce
1	can (4 oz.) diced green chiles, drained
1	can (2¼ oz.) sliced ripe olives, drained
4	eggs
½	pint (1 cup) sour cream
¼	teaspoon ground cumin
1½	cups (6 oz.) shredded Münster or jack cheese

Roll pastry out on a lightly floured board, then fit into a 10-inch pie pan. Flute edge. Bake in preheated 375° convection oven for 8 to 10 minutes or until crust begins to brown. Let cool on a wire rack. Reduce convection oven temperature to 350°.

Remove casings and crumble

sausage into a frying pan over medium-high heat. Cook, stirring, until meat is browned. With a slotted spoon, lift out meat; set aside. Pour off and discard all but 1 tablespoon drippings. Add onions to drippings and cook, stirring, for 1 minute; remove from heat. Stir in sausage, taco sauce, chiles, and olives; set aside.

In a bowl, beat eggs, sour cream, and cumin. Gently stir in sausage mixture and cheese; pour into partially baked pastry shell.

Bake in preheated 350° convection oven for 25 to 30 minutes or until crust is browned and a knife inserted just off center comes out clean. Let stand for 5 to 10 minutes. Makes 6 servings.

TUNA & SPROUT QUICHE

Make this tuna and sprout custard pie for a luncheon or light supper entrée. Bean sprouts give the quiche a pleasant, crunchy texture.

	Pastry for a single-crust 9-inch pie
	All-purpose flour
3	tablespoons butter or margarine
2	large onions, thinly sliced
¾	cup finely chopped celery
1½	cups chopped fresh bean sprouts
½	teaspoon thyme leaves
2	cups (8 oz.) shredded sharp Cheddar cheese
1	can (about 7 oz.) chunk tuna, drained
4	eggs
½	cup milk
1	teaspoon seasoned salt
⅛	teaspoon pepper

Roll pastry out on a lightly floured board, then fit into a 9-inch pie pan. Flute edge. Bake in preheated 375° convection oven for 8 to 10 minutes or until crust begins to brown. Let cool on a wire rack. Reduce convection oven temperature to 350°.

In a wide frying pan over medium-high heat, melt butter. Add onions and celery and cook, stirring, until onions are soft. Remove from heat and stir in bean sprouts and thyme. Sprinkle 1 cup of the cheese into partially baked pastry shell, then spoon half the onion mixture over cheese, and top with all of the tuna. Cover with remaining onion mixture and remaining 1 cup cheese. In a bowl, beat eggs, milk, salt, and pepper; pour into pastry shell.

Bake in preheated 350° convection oven for 30 to 35 minutes or until a knife inserted just off center comes out clean. Let stand for 5 to 10 minutes. Makes 6 servings.

CHILE HAM STRATA

This puffy baked sandwich is well suited to a family supper. You can prepare it in the morning and refrigerate it to be baked in the evening.

1   can (4 oz.) diced green chiles, drained
1   cup (about 4 oz.) finely chopped cooked ham
2   cups (8 oz.) shredded jack or sharp Cheddar cheese
8   slices day-old firm white bread
    Butter or margarine
6   eggs, lightly beaten
2   cups milk
½   teaspoon each chili powder and dry mustard

Mix chiles with ham and 1 cup of the cheese. Divide mixture into four equal parts and spread over four of the bread slices. Top with remaining slices to make four

sandwiches. Place in a well-buttered 9-inch-square baking pan. In a bowl, beat eggs with milk, chili powder, and mustard; pour mixture evenly over sandwiches. Cover and refrigerate for at least 2 hours or until next day.

Sprinkle sandwiches with remaining 1 cup cheese. Bake, uncovered, in 325° convection oven for 40 to 45 minutes or until egg mixture is set and sandwiches are puffed in center. Let stand for about 5 minutes before serving. Makes 4 servings.

CUSTARD CORNMEAL SQUARES

Though not a quiche, the vegetable-laden cheese filling may remind you of one. Cornbread makes an appealingly crisp crust. For a meatless meal, accompany it with an avocado and tomato salad.

1   package (15 oz.) cornbread mix
¾   teaspoon ground cumin
1⅔ cups milk
2   tablespoons butter or margarine
1   medium-size onion, finely chopped
1   small green pepper, seeded and chopped
1   cup whole kernel corn, cut off cob (about 2 ears), or frozen and thawed
1   can (4 oz.) diced green chiles, drained
½   teaspoon salt
1   teaspoon oregano leaves
3   eggs, lightly beaten
1   cup (4 oz.) shredded jack cheese

Combine cornbread mix, cumin, and ⅔ cup of the milk; press into bottom and 1½ inches up sides of a greased 9 by 13-inch baking pan; set aside.

In a frying pan over medium heat, melt butter. Add onion and green pepper and cook for 3 minutes. Stir corn, chiles, salt, and oregano into onion mixture and cook for 2 minutes; set aside.

In a large bowl, combine remaining 1 cup milk, eggs, and cheese; stir in vegetable mixture. Pour into cornbread crust.

Bake, uncovered, in preheated 350° convection oven for 20 to 30 minutes or until top and crust are well browned and a knife inserted in center comes out clean. Let stand for 10 minutes before cutting into squares. Makes 6 to 8 servings.

HAM & SOUR CREAM OVEN OMELET

Sauté apple slices to serve with this puffy omelet for a weekend brunch or supper.

5   eggs, separated
½   cup sour cream
3   tablespoons each chopped parsley and green onions (including tops)
1   cup finely diced cooked ham
1½ tablespoons butter or margarine
    Sour cream

In a bowl, beat egg whites until stiff, moist peaks form. In a large bowl, beat egg yolks until very

(Continued on page 67)

Oven pancakes are easy to whip up and spectacular to serve. This version, bursting with an onion-mushroom filling and two kinds of cheese, is served with sour cream and green onions for a super supper or brunch entrée. The recipe for mushroom-filled oven pancake is on page 69.

thick, then beat in the ½ cup sour cream. Stir parsley, onions, and ham into egg yolk mixture. Gently fold beaten whites into egg yolk mixture just until blended.

In an 8 or 10-inch frying pan with an ovenproof handle, melt butter over medium heat. Tilting pan, coat bottom and sides with butter. Pour egg mixture into pan and smooth surface gently. Reduce heat to low and cook until edges are lightly browned (7 to 10 minutes); to test, lift edge with spatula.

Bake in preheated 325° convection oven for 12 to 15 minutes or until top is golden and knife inserted in center comes out clean.

Run a spatula around edge of omelet, then tip pan and slide spatula underneath omelet to loosen. Slide omelet onto a heated plate. Separate into wedges with two forks, or cut gently with a knife. Serve with additional sour cream. Makes 4 servings.

EGG & CHEESE PUFFS

These individual egg entrées rise dramatically like soufflés, but they are much easier to make—simply beat eggs, combine with cheese, and bake. The puffs are a wonderful choice for brunch, with bacon and croissants.

- 6 eggs
- ½ cup half-and-half (light cream)
- 3 tablespoons all-purpose flour
- 1½ teaspoons dry mustard
- ¼ teaspoon salt
- ⅛ teaspoon ground white pepper
- 1½ cups (6 oz.) shredded sharp Cheddar cheese
  Butter or margarine

Preheat convection oven to 325°. With a rotary beater, beat eggs, half-and-half, flour, mustard, salt, and pepper. Evenly distribute cheese in four well buttered 10-ounce soufflé dishes or custard cups. Pour egg mixture evenly into dishes.

Bake in preheated 325° convection oven for 30 to 35 minutes or until tops are golden and puffy. Serve immediately. Makes 4 servings.

MEXICAN CHEESE PUFF

Unlike the short-lived soufflé, this flavorful egg dish holds its shape even if it stands for some time before serving. Sausage links, rolls, and sliced fresh oranges complete the menu for a perfect brunch buffet.

- 3½ cups (14 oz. each) shredded jack cheese and shredded sharp Cheddar cheese
- 1 large can (7 oz.) diced green chiles
- 2 medium-size tomatoes, seeded and chopped
- 1 can (2¼ oz.) sliced ripe olives, drained
- ½ cup all-purpose flour
- 6 eggs, separated
- 1 small can (5⅓ oz.) evaporated milk
- ½ teaspoon each salt and oregano leaves
- ¼ teaspoon each ground cumin and cream of tartar

Preheat convection oven to 300°. In a bowl, stir together jack and Cheddar cheeses, chiles, tomatoes, olives, and 2 tablespoons of the flour until well combined. Transfer mixture to a well greased shallow 3-quart baking pan.

In a small bowl, beat egg yolks. Add remaining 6 tablespoons flour to egg yolk mixture

alternately with milk; beat until smooth. Stir in salt, oregano, and cumin. In a large bowl, beat egg whites with cream of tartar until stiff, moist peaks form. Gently fold egg yolk mixture into beaten whites. Spoon egg mixture over cheese mixture in baking pan.

Bake, uncovered, in preheated 300° convection oven for 45 to 50 minutes or until top is golden brown and feels firm when touched. Let stand for about 10 minutes before serving. Makes 10 to 12 servings.

BAKED MUSHROOM FRITTATA

Originally an Italian creation, a frittata is a sort of omelet, laden with cheese and healthful fresh vegetables. This version—so good with red wine and sourdough bread—contains mushrooms, zucchini, and even salami (if you wish) under a golden cheese crust.

- 4 tablespoons butter or margarine
- ¾ pound mushrooms, thinly sliced
- 2 medium-size zucchini, sliced
- ¼ pound salami, diced (optional)
- 12 eggs
- ½ teaspoon salt
- 1 teaspoon each thyme and basil leaves
- ½ cup sliced green onions (including tops)
- 2 cups (8 oz.) shredded mozzarella or jack cheese
- 1 cup grated Parmesan cheese

In a large frying pan over medium-high heat, melt butter. Add mushrooms and zucchini and cook, stirring, until mushrooms are soft and liquid has evaporated. Remove from heat and stir in salami, if used.

In a bowl, beat eggs, salt, thyme, and basil. Stir in mushroom mixture; transfer to a well greased shallow 3-quart baking pan. Top with onions and mozzarella and Parmesan cheeses.

Bake, uncovered, in 350° convection oven for 30 minutes or until a knife inserted in center comes out clean. Let stand for about 5 minutes before cutting into squares. Makes 8 to 10 servings.

PUFFY SPROUT FRITTATA

Bean sprouts abound in this frittata, which is baked in an ovenproof frying pan that can be brought to the table. If you don't have such a pan, start with a regular frying pan; then, when ready to bake, transfer the frittata to a greased and heated 2-quart (about 9-inch-square) baking pan.

¾ cup sour cream
10 eggs
1 teaspoon salt
¼ teaspoon pepper
2 teaspoons dry basil
2 tablespoons chopped parsley
⅛ teaspoon ground red pepper (cayenne)
3 tablespoons butter or margarine
½ cup chopped green onions (including tops)
¼ pound mushrooms, sliced
½ pound bean sprouts
4 or 5 strips bacon, crisply cooked, drained, and crumbled (optional)
¼ cup grated Parmesan cheese
Tomato slices and parsley sprigs

In a large bowl, beat sour cream until smooth; add eggs, one at a time, beating well after each addition. Stir in salt, pepper, basil, parsley, and red pepper; set aside.

In an 8 or 10-inch frying pan with an ovenproof handle, melt butter over medium heat. Add onions, mushrooms, and sprouts and cook, stirring, until sprouts are limp (about 5 minutes); remove from heat. Sprinkle bacon, if used, over vegetables and pour in egg mixture. Sprinkle with cheese.

Bake, uncovered, in 350° convection oven for 25 to 35 minutes or until well browned, puffy, and a knife inserted in center comes out clean. Let stand for at least 5 minutes. Serve hot or at room temperature, garnished with tomato slices and parsley. Makes 6 servings.

GIANT OVEN PANCAKE

Descended from the popover by way of Yorkshire pudding, pancakes such as this one are also known as Dutch babies. If you wish, you can make the batter an hour or two ahead and refrigerate it until you're ready to bake the pancake. It's good for breakfast, lunch, or a light supper.

Though we like to dust the pancake with powdered sugar and squeeze a little lemon juice over it, you can choose your own toppings from among a long list of possibilities: warm honey, maple or fruit syrup, strawberries, sliced peaches, blueberries, or sautéed apples and sour cream.

¼ cup butter or margarine
3 eggs
¾ cup each milk and all-purpose flour
Powdered sugar
Lemon wedges

Place butter in a 2 to 3-quart round or oval shallow baking pan or frying pan with ovenproof handle and set in convection oven while it preheats to 375°.

Meanwhile, place eggs in a blender or food processor; whirl at high speed for 1 minute. With motor running, gradually pour in milk, then slowly add flour; continue whirling for 30 more seconds. Or, in a bowl, beat eggs until blended; gradually beat in milk, then slowly beat in flour.

When butter is melted, remove pan from oven and pour in batter. Return to convection oven and bake for 20 to 25 minutes or until pancake is puffy and well browned. Cut into wedges and serve immediately. Offer powdered sugar and lemon wedges at the table. Makes 3 servings.

SWISS CUSTARD RAMEKINS

This make-ahead dish is kin to both cheese fondue and quiche: a white wine-cheese custard saturates the buttered bread base and puffs it up. The result is an unusual hot sandwich to serve with smoky sausage links.

4 slices day-old firm white bread
Butter or margarine, softened
2 cups (8 oz.) shredded Swiss cheese
3 eggs
1½ cups half-and-half (light cream) or milk
½ cup dry white wine
⅛ teaspoon each salt and dry mustard
2 green onions (including tops), finely chopped (optional)

Spread bread with butter and place in four well-buttered shallow ramekins (1½ to 2-cup size) or small baking pans. Distribute ½ cup of the cheese over each bread slice. In a bowl, beat eggs with half-and-half, wine, salt, and mustard. Pour egg mixture over cheese. If desired, sprinkle with onions. Cover and refrigerate for at least 30 minutes or until next day.

Bake, uncovered, in 350° convection oven for 20 to 25 minutes or until custard is set and sandwiches puff up. Serve immediately. Makes 4 servings.

VEGETABLE CHEESE SQUARES

This cheese and vegetable dish combines many flavors of a summer harvest. Serve it as an entrée with soup or salad, or serve it as a casserole with meat.

¼ cup salad oil
1 small eggplant (about 1 lb.), peeled and coarsely chopped
1 medium-size onion, coarsely chopped
1 clove garlic, minced or pressed
1 small zucchini, thinly sliced
3 large mushrooms, thinly sliced
¾ teaspoon each dry basil and oregano leaves
½ teaspoon salt
⅛ teaspoon pepper
3 large tomatoes, peeled and coarsely chopped
4 eggs
½ cup grated Parmesan cheese
2 cups (8 oz.) shredded mozzarella cheese
Paprika

Heat salad oil in a wide frying pan over medium heat. Add eggplant, onion, and garlic and cook, stirring occasionally, until vegetables are soft (about 10 minutes). Add zucchini, mush-rooms, basil, oregano, salt, and pepper, and cook until mushrooms are soft (about 7 minutes). Add tomatoes and simmer rapidly until all liquid has evaporated (about 15 minutes). Cool.

Beat eggs lightly; combine with ¼ cup of the Parmesan cheese. Stir into cooled eggplant mixture. Pour half of this into a well-greased 8-inch-square baking pan. Top with half the mozzarella cheese, then top with remaining vegetable mixture. Sprinkle with remaining cheeses, then lightly with paprika.

Bake, uncovered, in a 350° convection oven for 18 to 20 minutes or until puffed and browned. Cool on rack for 10 minutes, then cut in squares. Makes 4 to 6 servings.

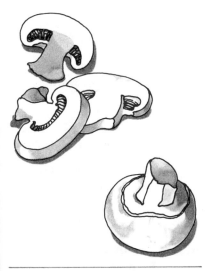

MUSHROOM-FILLED OVEN PANCAKE

Pictured on page 66

Adding mushrooms, onion, and seasonings to an oven pancake makes it into a substantial treat for a family supper. Instead of forming a concave hollow in the center like the giant oven pancake shown on the facing page, this version puffs up and stays puffy when you serve it.

If you don't have a large frying pan with an ovenproof handle, you can prepare the filling in another frying pan as directed, then transfer the filling to a 9 by 13-inch baking pan or shallow oval 3-quart pan.

About 7 tablespoons butter or margarine
½ pound mushrooms, sliced
1 small onion, chopped
1 teaspoon dry basil
½ teaspoon salt
⅛ teaspoon each pepper and ground nutmeg
4 eggs
1 cup each milk and all-purpose flour
1 cup (4 oz.) shredded Cheddar cheese or ⅓ cup grated Parmesan cheese
Sour cream
Thinly sliced green onions

In a 10-inch frying pan with an ovenproof handle, melt 3 tablespoons of the butter over medium heat. Add mushrooms and onion and cook, stirring, until mushrooms begin to brown. Stir in basil, salt, pepper, and nutmeg. Tip pan to estimate drippings, then add more butter (usually about 4 tablespoons) to drippings to make about 5 tablespoons. Place pan in 375° convection oven until butter melts and bubbles.

Meanwhile, in a blender or food processor, whirl eggs for 1 minute. With motor running, gradually pour in milk, then slowly add flour; whirl for 30 more seconds. Or, in a bowl, beat eggs until blended; gradually beat in milk, then slowly beat in flour.

Remove pan from convection oven, quickly pour in batter, sprinkle with cheese, and return to convection oven. Bake for 20 to 30 minutes or until puffy and well browned. Serve immediately. Offer sour cream and onions at the table to spoon over individual servings. Makes 4 servings.

Breads

This chapter is a veritable bread cook book in itself. We were so excited about the quality of convection-baked breads that we couldn't resist including an extensive selection of both yeast breads and quick breads—one recipe just led to another!

Thanks to the even temperature and circulating hot air of convection oven cooking, yeast breads bake high and even-textured, with superbly browned, crisp crusts. All kinds of quick breads, too, turn out evenly browned, light-textured, and tasty. Fruit and nut breads (quick breads) turn out moist and scrumptious.

We found that breads generally bake faster in metal pans than in glass or ceramic containers, and our recipes are timed for metal pans.

You could probably start your own bakery with the variety of yeast rising breads we've featured in this chapter. Recipes range from a super simple white bread (page 80) to chal-lah (braided egg bread—page 77), and yeast-rising sweet breads.

The cornucopia of quick breads in this chapter includes crisp, brown Cheddar cheese popovers (page 73), a spectacular cheese puff ring (page 75), and recipes for all kinds of fruit and nut muffins and breads, not to mention three quick coffee cakes.

Adapting your own recipes. Fruit and nut breads in a convection oven bake best at 300°—about 50° lower than the temperature you'd use in a standard oven. Bake your favorite fruit or nut breads for the same time specified in your standard recipe, but then test by inserting a wooden pick in the center. If it comes out clean, the bread is done; if not, let it bake for 10 to 15 more minutes. Quick coffee cakes, too, bake best at temperatures about 50° lower than those given in standard recipes. But they aren't as dense and moist as fruit and nut quick breads, so they'll probably be done in the same length of time suggested in your favorite recipes.

To adapt recipes for yeast-rising loaves for convection baking, lower the temperature 25° to 50°. Rich, dense loaves bake best at lower temperatures; the time should be about the same.

The usual test for doneness is to bake bread until it's golden brown, then tap the loaf—when it sounds hollow, it's done.

Proofing bread in a convection oven. If your convection oven can be set very low—and most of them can—then you may want to use it as a chamber for "proofing" a yeast dough (letting it rise). Check your oven with a reliable oven thermometer to find the setting that will establish a temperature between 90° and 100°. Then place the dough in a bowl, cover it, and let it rise in the warm oven for the time specified in your recipe.

Here it is: The definitive state-of-the-art loaf of bread. Outside, the crust is perfectly browned and crisp; inside, the bread is tender and even-textured—and that's what convection-baked breads are all about. The recipe for this magnificent braided egg bread, the traditional Jewish <u>challah</u>, is on page 77.

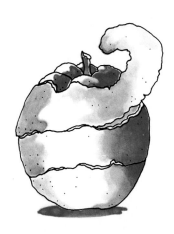

THREE-WAY QUICK NUT LOAVES

Depending on the season, this moist nut bread can be made with oranges, apples, or zucchini. Whatever the flavor, the bread will be easier to slice if it stands for at least a day. Wrapped well, it keeps in the refrigerator for up to a week, or you can freeze it for longer storage.

- **2 cups orange, apple, or zucchini mixture (recipes follow)**
- **3 cups all-purpose flour**
- **1 teaspoon each salt and baking soda**
- **½ teaspoon baking powder**
- **2 teaspoons ground cinnamon**
- **1 cup chopped walnuts**
- **3 eggs**
- **1½ cups sugar**
- **1 cup salad oil**
- **1 teaspoon vanilla**

Make orange, apple, or zucchini mixture.

In a bowl, combine flour, salt, soda, baking powder, cinnamon, and nuts; set aside. In a large bowl, beat eggs lightly; add sugar and oil and stir until blended. Stir in vanilla and orange, apple, or zucchini mixture. Add flour mixture all at once and stir just until evenly moistened. Spread batter into 2 greased and floured 4½ by 8½-inch loaf pans.

Bake in preheated 300° convection oven for 1 to 1¼ hours or until a wooden pick inserted in center comes out clean. Let stand in pans for 10 minutes, then turn out on wire racks to cool completely. Wrap well and refrigerate or freeze. Makes 2 loaves.

Orange mixture. From 4 large **oranges**, grate 1 tablespoon orange peel then cut off and discard remaining peel plus all the white membrane. Remove seeds (if any) and finely chop pulp; you should have 2 cups. Combine pulp and grated peel.

Apple mixture. Peel, core, and shred 3 or 4 medium-size tart **apples**; you should have 2 cups. Stir 1 teaspoon **lemon juice** into apple.

Zucchini mixture. Coarsely shred about 2 medium-size **zucchini**; you should have 2 cups (packed lightly).

CRANBERRY ORANGE MUFFINS

Colorful, nut-crusted muffins such as these are a delightful addition to an autumn brunch or lunch. If made ahead, wrap them loosely in foil and reheat in a 350° convection oven for about 10 minutes.

- **Nut topping (recipe follows)**
- **2 cups all-purpose flour**
- **¼ cup sugar**
- **3 teaspoons baking powder**
- **½ teaspoon each baking soda and salt**
- **1 egg**
- **¼ cup salad oil**
- **1 cup orange juice**
- **1 teaspoon grated orange peel**
- **1 cup cranberries, coarsely chopped**

Prepare nut topping; set aside.

Grease twelve 2½-inch muffin cups or line them with paper baking cups. In a large bowl, combine flour, sugar, baking powder, soda, and salt; make a well in center. In another bowl, beat egg lightly and stir in oil, orange juice, peel, and cranberries. Pour all at once into well in flour. Stir just until moistened; mixture should be lumpy. Quickly spoon batter into prepared muffin cups, filling each about two-thirds full. Sprinkle tops evenly with nut topping.

Bake in preheated 325° convection oven for 20 to 25 minutes or until well browned. Turn out on a wire rack. Makes 12 muffins.

Nut topping. In a bowl, mix together ¼ cup firmly packed **brown sugar**, ⅓ cup chopped **walnuts** or almonds, and ½ teaspoon **ground cinnamon**.

WHOLE WHEAT BANANA MUFFINS

These wholesome muffins have a wheaty flavor that is not too sweet. Serve them freshly baked for a special breakfast treat.

- **¾ cup all-purpose flour**
- **½ cup whole wheat flour**
- **¼ cup wheat germ**
- **2 tablespoons sugar**
- **1½ teaspoons baking powder**
- **½ teaspoon baking soda**
- **¼ teaspoon salt**
- **⅛ teaspoon ground cinnamon**
- **1 egg**
- **½ cup milk**
- **½ cup mashed ripe banana (about 1 medium-size banana)**
- **¼ cup salad oil**

Grease twelve 2½-inch muffin cups or line them with paper baking cups.

In a large bowl, combine all-purpose flour, whole wheat flour, wheat germ, sugar, baking powder, soda, salt, and cinnamon. In another bowl, beat egg with milk; mix in banana and oil. Add banana mixture to flour mixture and stir just until evenly blended. Spoon into prepared muffin cups, filling each about two-thirds full.

Bake in preheated 325° convection oven for 20 to 25 minutes or until a wooden pick inserted in center comes out clean. Turn out on a wire rack. Makes 12 muffins.

RAISIN BREAKFAST BREAD

Serve this quick loaf right out of the oven with butter or cream cheese. Or try it thinly sliced and toasted.

- 1 cup raisins
- 1 cup boiling water
- ¼ cup shortening
- 1 teaspoon vanilla
- 1 cup sugar
- 2 eggs
- 2 cups all-purpose flour
- 3 teaspoons baking powder
- ½ teaspoon salt
- ½ cup chopped walnuts

Place raisins in a small bowl. Pour boiling water over raisins and let stand until cool. In a large bowl, beat shortening and vanilla until creamy; gradually add sugar, beating until light and fluffy. Add eggs, one at a time, beating well after each addition. In another bowl, combine flour, baking powder, and salt. Add flour mixture to creamed mixture alternately with raisin and water mixture, mixing just until blended after each addition. Stir in nuts. Spread in a greased, flour-dusted 4½ by 8½-inch loaf pan.

Bake in preheated 300° convection oven for 1 to 1¼ hours or until a wooden pick inserted in center comes out clean. Let cool slightly, then remove from pan. Makes 1 loaf.

GRANOLA PEACH LOAF

This crusty fresh peach bread is studded with almonds and granola. Nectarines can be substituted for the peaches, if you wish.

-   3 or 4 ripe peaches or nectarines, peeled and pitted
- 1¾ cups all-purpose flour
- 1 teaspoon baking powder
- ½ teaspoon each salt and baking soda
- 1 teaspoon grated orange peel
- ⅔ cup granola-type cereal
- ½ cup chopped almonds or walnuts
- 6 tablespoons butter or margarine, softened
- ⅔ cup sugar
- 2 eggs
- 1 teaspoon vanilla
- 3 tablespoons orange juice

In a blender or food processor, whirl or process enough peaches to make 1 cup purée; set aside.

In a bowl, combine flour, baking powder, salt, and soda; add orange peel, cereal, and nuts. In another bowl, beat butter and sugar until creamy. Add eggs and beat until well blended; stir in vanilla, orange juice, and peach purée. Add flour mixture and mix just until blended. Pour batter into a well-greased, flour-dusted 5 by 9-inch loaf pan.

Bake in preheated 300° convection oven for 50 to 60 minutes or until a wooden pick inserted in center comes out clean. Let stand in pan for about 10 min-

utes, then turn out on a wire rack to cool completely. Wrap well and refrigerate or freeze. Makes 1 loaf.

CHEDDAR CHEESE POPOVERS

Pictured on page 31

Dramatically puffed and crisp, these popovers are a delightful addition to a meal. Try them with Mexican seasoning and olives, or just cheese. You can make the batter an hour or two in advance and refrigerate it until you're ready to bake the popovers.

- 1 cup all-purpose flour
- ½ teaspoon Mexican seasoning (optional)
- ½ teaspoon salt or garlic salt
- 1 tablespoon butter or margarine, melted
- 1 cup milk
- 3 eggs
- 1 cup (4 oz.) shredded sharp Cheddar cheese
- ¼ cup finely chopped ripe olives (optional)

In a large bowl, blender, or food processor, combine flour, Mexican seasoning, and salt. Add butter, milk, and eggs; beat, whirl, or process until very smooth, scraping sides of bowl or blender frequently. Stir in cheese and olives, if desired.

Pour into 12 to 14 well-greased ⅓ to ½-cup-size containers (muffin cups or cast iron popover pan), filling each one-half to two-thirds full.

(Continued on page 75)

Puff, puff—it's a cheese puff ring so crusty and appealingly brown you'll want to snatch it from the oven and eat it on the spot. Also known as gougère, this French quick bread is remarkably easy to make—you just add Swiss cheese to cream puff pastry and arrange scoops of dough in a ring. The recipe is on the facing page.

74 Breads

Bake in preheated 350° convection oven for 40 to 45 minutes or until well browned and firm to touch. If you like your popovers especially dry inside, loosen them from pan but leave sitting at an angle in cups. Pierce side of each popover with a skewer; let stand in convection oven with heat at lowest setting for 2 to 3 minutes. Remove from pans and serve immediately. Makes 12 to 14 popovers.

CHEESE PUFF RING

Pictured on page 74

Adding Swiss cheese to cream-puff pastry produces a spectacular bread, delicious at lunch with a mixed green salad and red wine, or at dinner with barbecued meats. This bread originated in France, where it is called gougère.

- 1 **cup milk**
- ¼ **cup butter or margarine**
- ½ **teaspoon salt**
  Dash of ground white pepper
- 1 **cup all-purpose flour**
- 4 **eggs**
- 1 **cup (4 oz.) shredded Swiss cheese**

Heat milk and butter in a 2-quart pan over medium heat; add salt and pepper. Bring to a rolling boil. Add flour all at once and stir until mixture leaves sides of pan and forms a ball (about 2 minutes). Remove from heat and, with a wooden spoon, beat in eggs, one at a time, until mixture is smooth and well blended. Beat in ½ cup of the cheese.

With an ice cream scoop or a large spoon, and using about three-quarters of the dough, make 7 equal mounds of dough, placing them in a circle on a greased baking sheet. (Each mound of dough should just touch the next one.) Using remaining dough, place a small mound on top of each larger mound. Sprinkle remaining ½ cup cheese over all.

Bake in preheated 350° convection oven for 40 to 50 minutes or until puffs are well browned and crisp. Serve immediately. Makes 7 puffs.

GRAHAM YOGURT BREAD

Baked in three 1-pound fruit or vegetable cans (not coffee cans), these small round loaves are a handy size for quick snacks. They keep well—just wrap them airtight and refrigerate for as long as five days, or freeze for longer storage.

- 2 **cups graham flour or whole wheat flour**
- ½ **cup all-purpose flour**
- 2 **teaspoons baking soda**
- 1 **teaspoon salt**
- 1 **pint (2 cups) unflavored yogurt**
- ½ **cup molasses**
- 1 **cup raisins**
- ½ **cup chopped walnuts**

In a large bowl, combine graham flour, all-purpose flour, soda, and salt. Add yogurt, molasses, raisins, and walnuts; mix well. Divide batter evenly into 3 well-greased 1-pound cans with 1 end removed.

Bake in preheated 325° convection oven for 40 to 45 minutes or until a wooden pick inserted in center comes out clean. Let stand in cans for about 10 minutes, then turn out on a wire rack to cool completely. Makes 3 small loaves.

CARROT CORNBREAD

Carrots contribute golden flecks and moist texture to this cornbread. It's especially easy to make if you use your blender or food processor to chop or grate the carrots.

- 3 **tablespoons butter or margarine**
  About 2 medium-size carrots
- 1 **cup buttermilk**
- 1 **egg**
- 1 **cup yellow cornmeal**
- ½ **teaspoon each salt, baking powder, and baking soda**

Place butter in an 8-inch-square baking pan in convection oven while it preheats to 350°. When butter is melted, remove pan and set aside.

Peel carrots and cut into ½-inch slices; you should have about 1 cup. Place in a blender or food processor and whirl or process until finely chopped or grated. Add buttermilk and egg; whirl or process until blended.

In a bowl, combine cornmeal, salt, baking powder, and soda. Pour carrot mixture all at once into cornmeal mixture and stir until well blended. Add melted butter, leaving enough in pan to coat it well; stir batter until blended. Pour into baking pan.

Bake in preheated 350° convection oven for 20 to 25 minutes or until bread is browned and beginning to pull away from sides of pan. Cut in squares and serve warm. Makes about 6 servings.

Coconut topping. Combine ⅓ cup <u>each</u> firmly packed **brown sugar**, chopped **walnuts** or pecans, and **flaked coconut**. Add 2 teaspoons **ground cinnamon**, 2 tablespoons **all-purpose flour** and 2 tablespoons **butter** or margarine (softened); mix until crumbly.

OATMEAL COFFEE BREAD

Orange peel flavors this breakfast bread, topped with coconut, cinnamon, and nuts.

    Coconut topping (recipe follows)
¾ cup sugar
6 tablespoons butter or margarine, softened
2 eggs
1½ cups all-purpose flour
2 teaspoons baking powder
½ teaspoon salt
½ cup milk
½ cup rolled oats
1 tablespoon grated orange peel

In a small bowl, prepare coconut topping. In a large bowl, beat sugar and butter until creamy. Add eggs and beat well. In another bowl, combine flour, baking powder, and salt; add to egg mixture alternately with milk, stirring well after each addition. Stir in oats and orange peel. Spread in a greased 9-inch-square baking pan. Sprinkle evenly with coconut topping.

Bake in preheated 325° convection oven for 25 to 30 minutes or until a wooden pick inserted in center comes out clean. Makes 9 to 12 servings.

CARAMEL-TOPPED COFFEE CAKE

Here's a quick breakfast treat made with a few simple ingredients and drizzled with a caramel topping.

1 cup all-purpose flour
½ cup sugar
1½ teaspoons baking powder
½ teaspoon salt
1 teaspoon ground cinnamon
1 egg
½ cup milk
1 teaspoon vanilla
¼ cup butter or margarine, melted
    Caramel topping (recipe follows)
⅓ cup sliced almonds, chopped pecans, or chopped walnuts

In a large bowl, combine flour, sugar, baking powder, salt, and cinnamon. In another bowl, beat egg with milk. Stir in vanilla and melted butter; add to flour mixture and stir just until evenly blended. Spread in a greased 8-inch-square baking pan.

Bake in preheated 300° convection oven for 20 to 25 minutes or until wooden pick inserted in center comes out clean.

Meanwhile, prepare caramel topping. Remove cake from oven; drizzle with topping and sprinkle with nuts. Raise convection oven temperature to 350°, return cake to oven, and bake for 5 to 8 more minutes or

until nuts are toasted. Makes about 6 servings.

Caramel topping. In a small pan over medium heat combine 2 tablespoons <u>each</u> **butter** or margarine and **brown sugar**, 1 tablespoon **granulated sugar,** and a dash of **ground cinnamon**. Cook, stirring, until bubbly and syrupy; use immediately.

SOUR CREAM COFFEE CAKE

Baked in a tube pan, this tender, moist cake provides a sweet finale to a weekend brunch.

1 cup (½ lb.) butter or margarine, softened
1 cup granulated sugar
1 teaspoon vanilla
2 eggs
½ pint (1 cup) sour cream
2 cups all-purpose flour
1 teaspoon <u>each</u> baking powder and baking soda
¼ teaspoon salt
½ cup <u>each</u> coarsely chopped walnuts and firmly packed brown sugar
1 teaspoon ground cinnamon
1½ tablespoons vanilla blended with 1 tablespoon water
    Powdered sugar

In a large bowl, beat butter and granulated sugar until light and fluffy; add the 1 teaspoon vanilla. Add eggs, one at a time, beating well after each addition. Stir in sour cream. In another bowl, combine flour, baking powder, soda, and salt; blend into egg mixture.

In a small bowl, combine nuts, brown sugar, and cinnamon. Spoon a third of the batter into a greased, flour-dusted 9-inch (9 to 10-cup) tube pan; sprinkle with a third of the nut mixture. Continue layering two more times, ending with nut mixture.

Drizzle vanilla mixture over top.

Bake in preheated 300° convection oven for 1 to 1¼ hours or until a wooden pick inserted in center comes out clean. Let cool in pan on a wire rack for 20 minutes, then remove from pan. Dust with powdered sugar. Makes 8 to 10 servings.

NUT CRUMB COFFEE CAKE

This light-textured coffee cake is a dramatic-looking creation; bake it in a 10-inch tube pan to show it off to its best advantage.

2	packages active dry yeast
½	cup warm water (about 110°)
1	cup milk, scalded
1	cup granulated sugar
1	teaspoon salt
2	eggs
¾	cup butter or margarine, melted and cooled
5	cups all-purpose flour
⅓	cup graham cracker crumbs
1	cup chopped walnuts, filberts, almonds, or pecans
1	teaspoon each grated orange peel and ground cinnamon
	Powdered sugar

In a small bowl, dissolve yeast in warm water. In a large bowl, combine milk, ⅔ cup of the granulated sugar, and salt; let stand until lukewarm. Beat in yeast mixture, eggs, ½ cup of the butter, and 2 cups of the flour until smooth. Beat in remaining 3 cups flour until dough is elastic. Place the dough in a greased bowl, cover, and let rise until doubled (about 1 hour). Meanwhile, combine cracker crumbs, nuts, orange peel, cinnamon, and remaining ⅓ cup granulated sugar.

Punch dough down; spoon out walnut-size balls of dough and roll each in remaining ¼ cup melted butter. Arrange in a greased 10-inch tube pan. After a third of the dough is shaped, sprinkle balls with a third of the crumb mixture. Repeat layering 2 more times. Let rise in a warm place until dough has risen above rim of pan (30 to 45 minutes).

Bake in preheated 300° convection oven for 40 to 50 minutes or until bread is well browned and sounds hollow when tapped. Let stand in pan for 10 minutes, then turn out of pan on a wire rack to cool completely. Sprinkle with powdered sugar. Makes 1 large coffee cake.

SWEET OR SAVORY QUICK CRESCENTS

For a sweet morning treat, fill these buttery rolls with peach or apricot jam and nuts; for savory dinner rolls, flavor them with Parmesan cheese and herbs.

1	cup (½ lb.) butter or margarine
1	package active dry yeast
¼	cup warm water (about 110°)
2	tablespoons sugar
3	egg yolks, lightly beaten
1	can (5 oz.) evaporated milk
3⅓	cups all-purpose flour
	About 6 tablespoons peach or apricot jam and ¾ cup chopped nuts, or 6 tablespoons grated Parmesan cheese and 3 teaspoons dry basil or oregano leaves

In a small pan over medium heat, melt butter; let stand until lukewarm. In a large bowl, dissolve yeast in warm water; stir

in sugar, egg yolks, milk, and butter. Add flour and mix well. Cover and refrigerate for 8 hours or until next day.

Divide dough into 3 equal portions. On a floured board, roll out each portion to a 12-inch circle. For sweet rolls, spread each circle with 2 tablespoons of the jam and sprinkle with ¼ cup of the nuts. For savory rolls, sprinkle each circle with 2 tablespoons of the Parmesan and 1 teaspoon of the basil. With a sharp knife, cut each circle into 12 wedges. Roll each wedge from wide end toward point and place point side down, on greased baking sheets, leaving 2 inches between rolls. Curve into crescent shapes.

Bake in preheated 325° convection oven for 20 to 25 minutes or until golden. Turn out on wire racks to cool. Makes 3 dozen crescents.

BRAIDED EGG BREAD

Pictured on page 71

This spectacular braided bread, sprinkled with sesame seeds or poppy seeds, is the traditional Jewish Sabbath and holiday loaf known as challah.

1	package active dry yeast
1¼	cups warm water (about 110°)
1	teaspoon salt
¼	cup each sugar and salad oil
2	eggs, lightly beaten
	Pinch of saffron (optional)
	4¾ to 5 cups all-purpose flour
1	egg yolk beaten with 1 tablespoon water
	About 1 tablespoon sesame seeds or poppy seeds

In a large bowl, dissolve yeast in water. Stir in salt, sugar, oil, eggs, and saffron (if desired). Gradually beat in about 4½ cups of the flour to form a stiff dough. Turn out on a floured board and knead until smooth and satiny (5 to 20 minutes), adding remaining flour as needed to prevent sticking. Turn dough over in a greased bowl; cover and let rise in a warm place until doubled (1¼ to 1½ hours).

Punch dough down; knead briefly on a lightly floured board just to expel air. Tear off about ¾ cup of the dough; cover and set aside.

Divide remaining dough into 4 equal portions. Rolling each portion between your hands, form a strip about 18 inches long. Place 4 strips lengthwise on a greased baking sheet, pinch tops together, and braid as follows: pick up strand on right, bring it over next one, under the third, and over the fourth. Repeat, always starting with strand on right, until braid is complete. Pinch ends together.

Roll reserved dough into a strand about 18 inches long; cut into three 6-inch strips and braid. Arrange over center of large braid. Cover and let rise in a warm place until almost doubled (45 to 60 minutes).

With a soft brush, paint egg yolk mixture evenly over braids; sprinkle with seeds. Bake in preheated 325° convection oven for 30 to 40 minutes or until loaf is golden brown and sounds hollow when tapped. Turn out on a wire rack to cool. Makes 1 large loaf.

POTATO CINNAMON BUNS

Pictured on page 79

You can make plump cinnamon rolls from a traditional potato dough. For added appeal, drizzle the tops with a cinnamon-flavored nut glaze.

½ pound thick-skinned potatoes
    Boiling water
1 cup milk
½ cup (¼ lb.) butter or margarine
½ cup sugar
½ teaspoon salt
1 package active dry yeast
1 tablespoon sugar
¼ cup warm water (about 110°)
4½ to 5 cups all-purpose flour
1 egg
1 teaspoon vanilla
    Cinnamon filling (recipe follows)
    Nut glaze (recipe follows)

In a saucepan over medium heat, cook potatoes in boiling water until tender when pierced (25 to 35 minutes). Drain, peel, and mash with a potato masher or press through a potato ricer; you should have 1 cup mashed potatoes.

Put potatoes in clean pan and gradually pour in milk, stirring, until mixture is smooth and well blended. Add 4 tablespoons of the butter, the ½ cup sugar, and salt; warm over low heat, stirring, until lukewarm (about 110°).

In a large bowl, dissolve yeast and the 1 tablespoon sugar in warm water. Let stand until bubbly (about 10 minutes). Add potato mixture, 2 cups of the flour, egg, and vanilla; beat until smooth and well blended. Gradually stir in 2 cups more flour. Turn out on a heavily floured board and knead until smooth and elastic (about 15 minutes), adding remaining flour as needed to prevent sticking. Turn dough over in a greased bowl; cover and let rise in a warm place until doubled (1 to 1¼ hours). Meanwhile, prepare cinnamon filling.

Melt remaining 4 tablespoons butter. Punch dough down; knead just to expel air. Roll dough out to a 15 by 18-inch

rectangle. Brush with 3 tablespoons of the melted butter and sprinkle with cinnamon filling. Starting at wide end, roll up, jelly-roll fashion; cut into 12 equal pieces, each about 1½ inches thick. Place pieces, cut side down, in a greased 9 by 13-inch baking pan. Brush remaining 1 tablespoon melted butter over rolls. Cover and let rise in a warm place until almost doubled (35 to 45 minutes).

Bake rolls in preheated 325° convection oven for 30 to 40 minutes or until richly browned. Meanwhile prepare nut glaze. Drizzle with nut glaze. Makes 12 rolls.

Cinnamon filling. In a small bowl, combine ½ cup firmly packed **brown sugar,** ¼ cup **granulated sugar,** and 3 teaspoons **ground cinnamon.** If desired, add ½ cup **raisins.**

Nut glaze. In a bowl, combine 1½ cups unsifted **powdered sugar,** ¼ cup chopped **nuts,** ⅛ teaspoon **ground cinnamon,** 1 tablespoon melted **butter** or margarine, and 2 to 2½ tablespoons **water.**

CINNAMON-SWIRL LOAF

Cinnamon, sugar, and raisins swirl through each slice of this delicious bread.

1 package active dry yeast
¼ cup warm water (about 110°)
½ cup <u>each</u> milk and sugar
4 tablespoons butter or margarine
¾ teaspoon salt
    About 3 cups all-purpose flour
1 egg
¾ cup raisins
1 tablespoon ground cinnamon

(Continued on page 80)

An old-fashioned yeast-rising potato dough gives these plump potato cinnamon buns their special tenderness. They're chock-full of cinnamon and raisins and drizzled with a nut glaze—irresistible, especially when still warm from the oven and slathered with butter. The recipe is on the facing page.

Breads **79**

In a large bowl, dissolve yeast in warm water. In a pan, combine milk, ¼ cup of the sugar, butter, and salt. Stirring, warm over low heat; stir into yeast mixture. Add 1½ cups of the flour, along with egg and raisins; beat for 3 minutes. Stir in 1 cup more flour. Turn out on a floured board; knead for 5 minutes, adding remaining flour as needed to prevent sticking. Turn dough over in a greased bowl; cover and let rise in a warm place until doubled (1 to ½ hours).

Punch dough down. Roll dough out to a 9 by 18-inch rectangle. Mix remaining ¼ cup sugar with cinnamon; sprinkle over dough. Starting at narrow end, roll up tightly. Place in a greased 5 by 9-inch loaf pan. Cover and let rise in a warm place until nearly doubled (about 1 hour).

Bake in preheated 325° convection oven for 40 to 45 minutes or until crust is golden brown and bread sounds hollow when tapped. Turn out on a wire rack to cool. Makes 1 loaf.

SUPER SIMPLE WHITE BREAD

Making bread couldn't be easier. There's no kneading and the dough rests in the refrigerator.

⅓ cup <u>each</u> sugar and shortening
3 teaspoons salt
2 cups boiling water
2 packages active dry yeast
1 teaspoon sugar
¼ cup warm water (about 110°)
2 eggs
7½ to 8 cups all-purpose flour

In a large bowl, combine the ⅓ cup sugar, shortening, salt, and boiling water; let stand until lukewarm. In a small bowl, dissolve yeast and the 1 teaspoon sugar in the ¼ cup warm water; let stand until bubbly (5 to 10 minutes). Add to lukewarm mixture. Beat in eggs. With a wooden spoon, beat in 4 cups of the flour; gradually add as much of the remaining flour as dough will absorb and mix well. Turn dough over in a greased bowl, cover and refrigerate for at least 3 hours or until next day.

Divide dough in half. With greased hands, shape into smooth loaves and place in 2 greased 5 by 9-inch loaf pans. Cover and let rise in a warm place until almost doubled (about 1½ hours).

Bake in preheated 325° convection oven for 30 to 35 minutes or until loaves are golden brown and sound hollow when tapped. Turn out on wire racks to cool. Makes 2 loaves.

ONION KULCHA

Kulcha—chewy, onion-flavored rolls from northern India—are traditionally baked on the walls of a bullet-shaped clay oven called a <u>tandoor</u>. We have adapted the recipe for the convection oven.

1 package active dry yeast
1 tablespoon sugar
¼ cup warm water (about 110°)
4 tablespoons butter or margarine, melted and cooled
¼ cup unflavored yogurt
1 cup water
1 egg
2 teaspoons salt
About 4½ cups all-purpose flour
3 tablespoons instant minced onion combined with 2 tablespoons water
1 tablespoon salad oil
Salad oil
Poppy seeds

In a large bowl, dissolve yeast and sugar in the ¼ cup warm water. Stir in butter, yogurt, the 1 cup water, egg, and salt. Add 2 cups of the flour, beating until smooth. Stir in 2½ cups more flour to form a soft dough. Turn out on a floured board and knead until smooth (about 10 minutes). Turn dough over in a greased bowl; cover and let rise in a warm place until doubled (about 1½ hours). Meanwhile, combine instant minced onion mixture with the 1 tablespoon oil.

Punch dough down and turn out on a floured board. Divide dough into 12 pieces. Shape each piece into a ball and press a rounded half teaspoon of onion mixture into center of each ball. Pull dough up over onions and pinch closed. Stretch and flatten each ball into a 6-inch-long oval. Place on 3 greased baking sheets (4 rolls on a sheet), brush with additional oil, and sprinkle lightly with poppy seeds. Let rise, uncovered, until puffy (about 10 minutes).

Place 1 baking sheet on lowest rack of preheated 350° convection oven and bake for 10 minutes. Move to highest rack and bake for 6 to 8 more minutes or until golden. Repeat with remaining 2 sheets. Turn out on wire racks to cool. Package airtight or freeze. Makes 12 rolls.

SOUR RYE BREAD

This remarkable bread, light and tender in texture, combines the hearty flavors of molasses, beer, fennel, and rye. Start the dough the night before you want to bake it, since it needs to stand at room temperature for at least 12 hours. You couldn't pick a better bread for corned beef or pastrami sandwiches, or to serve with hearty soups.

- 1   cup buttermilk
- 1   teaspoon grated orange peel
- ¾   cup beer
- ½   cup molasses
- 1½ teaspoons salt
- 1   teaspoon fennel seeds
- 1   package active dry yeast
- ¼   cup warm water (about 110°)
- 1½ cups rye flour
- ½   cup firmly packed brown sugar
- 1   tablespoon butter or margarine, softened
      About 5 cups all-purpose flour

In a small pan over medium heat, scald buttermilk with orange peel (milk will separate); pour into a large bowl. Stir in beer, molasses, salt, and fennel; let stand until lukewarm. In a small bowl, dissolve yeast in water; add to buttermilk mixture along with rye flour, stirring to blend. Cover and let stand at room temperature for at least 12 hours.

Next day, dough will be bubbly. Add brown sugar, butter, and 4½ cups of the all-purpose flour; stir until dough pulls away from sides of bowl. Turn out on a floured board and knead until smooth (about 15 minutes); adding remaining flour as needed. Turn dough over in a greased bowl, cover, and let rise in a warm place until it is almost doubled (1½ to 2 hours).

Punch dough down; knead just to expel air. Divide dough in half and shape into loaves. Place in 2 greased 4½ by 8½-inch loaf pans. Cover and let rise until almost doubled (45 to 60 minutes).

Bake in preheated 325° convection oven for 35 to 40 minutes or until richly browned. Let stand in pans for 10 minutes, then turn out on wire racks to cool completely. Makes 2 loaves.

WHOLE WHEAT RICOTTA ROLLS

Easy to make, these rolls combine the full-bodied flavor of whole wheat flour with the smoothness of ricotta cheese. Serve them with homemade soup for a cool-weather supper.

- 1   package active dry yeast
- ½   cup warm water (about 110°)
- 1   tablespoon honey
- ½   cup ricotta cheese (at room temperature)
- 1   tablespoon salad oil
- 1   egg
- 1   teaspoon salt
- 2   teaspoons dill seeds or caraway seeds (optional)
- 2   tablespoons instant minced onion
      About 2½ cups whole wheat flour

In a large bowl, dissolve yeast in warm water; blend in honey. Let stand until bubbly (about 15 minutes). Stir in cheese, oil, egg, salt, dill (if desired), and onion. Gradually beat in 2¼ cups of the flour to form a stiff dough. Turn out on a floured board and knead until smooth and no longer sticky, adding remaining flour as needed. Turn dough over in a greased bowl; cover and let rise in a warm place until doubled (about 1½ hours).

Punch dough down; knead just to expel air. Divide dough into 12 pieces and shape each piece into a ball. Place in a greased 9-inch round cake pan. Cover and let rise in a warm place until almost doubled (about 30 minutes).

Bake in preheated 325° convection oven for 20 to 25 minutes or until well browned. Cool on wire rack. Makes 12 rolls.

POTATO LOAVES

Fresh potatoes produce bread that is light and naturally sweet.

- 1   pound thick-skinned potatoes
- 1½ cups milk
- ⅓   cup butter or margarine
- ¼   cup sugar
- 2   teaspoons salt
- 2   packages active dry yeast
- ½   cup warm water (about 110°)
- 2   eggs
      About 8 cups all-purpose flour

In a saucepan over medium heat, cook potatoes in boiling water until tender when pierced (25 to 35 minutes). Drain, peel, and mash with a potato masher or press through a potato ricer; you should have 2 cups mashed potatoes. Put potatoes in clean pan and gradually stir in milk; add butter, sugar, and salt. Place over low heat until warm; set aside.

In a large bowl, dissolve yeast in the ½ cup warm water; let stand for 5 minutes. Beat in potato mixture, eggs, and 3 cups of the flour. Gradually beat in 3½ cups more flour. Turn out on a floured board and knead until smooth and elastic (about 10 minutes), adding remaining flour as needed. Turn dough over in a greased bowl; cover and let rise in a warm place until doubled (1 to 1½ hours).

Punch dough down; knead just to expel air. Divide dough in half and shape into smooth loaves. Place in 2 greased 5 by 9-inch loaf pans. Cover and let rise in a warm place until almost doubled (30 to 40 minutes).

Bake in preheated 325° convection oven for 35 to 40 minutes or until loaves are browned and sound hollow when tapped. Turn out on wire racks to cool. Makes 2 loaves.

Airy light but chocolate rich, this grated chocolate torte (recipe on page 85) is made with ground almonds and bread crumbs instead of flour; beaten egg whites provide the leavening. Serve it topped with whipped cream and chocolate curls, and get ready to answer your guests when they ask "Where did you buy that beautiful cake?"

Sweets

Bake up a batch of frosted apple cookies or walnut chews for the cooky monster in your house. Concoct an airy chocolate torte (page 85) to dazzle your guests. Or please the whole family with a moist chocolate cake or rhubarb apple berry pie (page 89). Convection cooking adapts easily to any kind of dessert, and you'll especially love the boost it gives desserts that need lightness and height—puff pastry, meringue, cream puffs, or a dessert soufflé.

Adapting your own recipes.
Most desserts bake at lower temperatures in a convection oven than in a standard oven. Desserts that contain leavening agents, such as baking powder, baking soda, or even air (incorporated in beaten eggs), bake best in a convection oven at temperatures 50° to 75° below those specified in recipes for standard ovens.

As a general rule, the richer and denser the dessert, the lower the convection oven temperature should be. For instance, moist chocolate cake (page 84) is baked in a convection oven at 275°F for 45 to 55 minutes. The same recipe would be baked in a standard oven 75° higher, at 350°F, for 40 minutes. If you tried to bake the cake in your convection oven at the higher temperature, the circulating hot air would cause a crust to form on top of the cake, and the bottom would not cook properly. The spiced apple cake (page 84), not as rich as the chocolate cake, bakes at a temperature 50° lower than the standard temperature for this type of apple cake.

Baking time for cakes generally stays about the same for both convection and standard recipes; convection baking may take slightly longer.

In general, pies are convection baked at a temperature 25° lower than that recommended for standard ovens; cookies are convection baked 50° to 75° lower than usual to prevent overbrowning. Baking time stays basically the same, or possibly just a minute or two longer for the convection oven.

See the adapting recipes chart on page 8 for convection cooking other desserts.

PEAR ALMOND TORTE

Pictured on page 87

Baked in a small bundt pan or other fluted tube pan, this fresh pear cake is moist and flavorful.

- 2 large ripe pears
- ½ cup (¼ lb.) butter or margarine, softened
- 1½ cups sugar
- 2 eggs
- 1 teaspoon vanilla
- ½ teaspoon almond extract
- 2 cups all-purpose flour
- 2 teaspoons baking soda
- 1 teaspoon ground cinnamon
- ½ teaspoon ground nutmeg
- ¼ teaspoon ground cloves
- ½ cup each raisins and chopped almonds
  Sliced almonds
  Orange glaze (recipe follows)

Core (but do not peel) and finely chop pears to make 2 cups. In a large bowl, beat butter and sugar together until creamy. Add eggs, one at a time, beating well after each addition until mixture is light and fluffy. Blend in vanilla, almond extract, and pears.

In a separate bowl, combine flour, soda, cinnamon, nutmeg, and cloves. Add to pear mixture and blend thoroughly. Stir in raisins and chopped almonds. Spread mixture in a well-greased, flour-dusted 2-quart tube pan.

Bake in preheated 300° convection oven for 1 hour and 10 to 20 minutes or until a wooden pick inserted in center comes out clean. Let stand in pan for 20 minutes; then turn out onto a wire rack to cool completely.

Spread almonds in a shallow pan and toast in a 350° convection oven for about 8 minutes or until lightly browned. Prepare orange glaze and drizzle over cake. Garnish with toasted almonds. Makes 10 to 12 servings.

Orange glaze. Combine 1 cup **powdered sugar,** ½ teaspoon grated **orange peel,** ¼ teaspoon **almond extract,** and 1½ tablespoons **orange juice.** Blend until smooth.

SPICED APPLE CAKE

Here is a moist, not overly sweet cake that goes well with coffee or milk any time.

- ½ cup (¼ lb.) butter or margarine, softened
- 1 cup firmly packed brown sugar
- 2 eggs
- ½ teaspoon vanilla
- 2 cups all-purpose flour
- 1¼ teaspoons baking soda
- ½ teaspoon baking powder
- 1 teaspoon ground cinnamon
- ¼ teaspoon salt
- ½ pint (1 cup) spiced apple yogurt
- ½ cup peeled, finely shredded apple
- ½ cup chopped walnuts or pecans
  Powdered sugar

In a large bowl, beat butter and brown sugar together until creamy. Add eggs and beat until fluffy; beat in vanilla. In a separate bowl, combine flour with soda, baking powder, cinnamon, and salt. Add to creamed mixture and mix to blend. Add yogurt and apple and mix just until blended. Stir in walnuts. Spread mixture in a greased, flour-dusted 2-quart tube pan.

Bake in preheated 300° convection oven for 40 to 50 min-utes or until a pick inserted in center comes out clean. Let stand in pan for 10 minutes; then turn out onto a wire rack to cool completely. Sprinkle with pow-dered sugar before serving. Makes 10 to 12 servings.

MOIST CHOCOLATE CAKE

This easy one-bowl chocolate cake is filled and frosted with a fluffy coffee-accented icing.

- ¼ cup cocoa
- 1 cup water
- 2 cups each all-purpose flour and sugar
- 1 teaspoon baking soda
- 1 cup (½ lb.) butter or margarine, melted and cooled
- ½ cup buttermilk
- 2 eggs
- 1 teaspoon vanilla
  Fluffy coffee icing (recipe follows)
  Chocolate sprinkles

Grease two 8-inch round cake pans; line bottoms with a circle of wax paper. Grease paper; then dust paper and pan sides with flour.

In a large bowl, blend cocoa and water. In a separate bowl, stir together flour, sugar, and soda; add to cocoa mixture and blend. Stir in butter, buttermilk, eggs, and vanilla. With an electric mixer, beat at medium speed for 2 minutes. Pour into prepared pans.

Bake in preheated 275° convection oven for 45 to 55 minutes or until edges of cake begin to pull away from pan sides. Let stand in pans for 10 minutes; then invert onto wire racks to cool completely.

Meanwhile, prepare icing and spread it between layers and over top and sides. Garnish with chocolate sprinkles. Let stand until softly set (at least 1 hour). Makes 9 to 12 servings.

Fluffy coffee icing. Place 2 **egg whites,** ½ cup **light corn syrup,** ½ cup firmly packed **brown sugar,** 1 teaspoon **instant coffee powder** or granules, and ⅛ teaspoon **salt** in top of double boiler. Beat just until mixed. Place over rapidly boiling water and cook, beating constantly, until frosting stands in peaks (3 to 4 minutes). Remove from heat and beat for 1 more minute. Beat in 1 teaspoon **vanilla.** Makes enough frosting for two 8-inch layers.

STREUSEL GINGER CAKE

You might bake this crunch-topped single layer cake as part of an oven meal, along with corned beef or the barbecue-style Swiss steak on page 16.

    Streusel topping (recipe follows)
1   egg
½   cup <u>each</u> sugar, salad oil, and light molasses
¼   cup boiling water
1¼ cups all-purpose flour
1   teaspoon baking soda
½   teaspoon ground ginger
¼   teaspoon ground cinnamon

Prepare streusel topping and set aside.

In a large bowl, beat egg until light and lemon-colored. Gradually beat in sugar, then oil, molasses, and water. In a separate bowl, combine flour, soda, ginger, and cinnamon. Add to molasses mixture and beat until smooth. Pour batter into a greased 9-inch-round cake pan. Sprinkle streusel evenly over top.

Bake in preheated 300° convection oven for 35 to 40 minutes or until a wooden pick

inserted in center comes out clean. Let stand in pan until cool, then cut into wedges. Makes 6 servings.

Streusel topping. Combine ¼ cup firmly packed **brown sugar,** 2 tablespoons **all-purpose flour,** 1 tablespoon melted **butter** or margarine, ¾ teaspoon **ground cinnamon,** and ¼ cup chopped **walnuts.** Mix until coarse crumbs form.

GRATED CHOCOLATE TORTE

Pictured on page 82

The airy tenderness of this chocolate-almond confection comes from beaten egg whites. For a spectacular presentation, the cake can be garnished with puffs of whipped cream and a shower of sweet chocolate curls. To make the curls, leave a large, thick chunk of milk chocolate at room temperature until chocolate just begins to glisten; then shave the curls with a cheese plane or vegetable peeler.

1   cup (½ lb.) butter or margarine, softened
1   cup powdered sugar
6   eggs, separated
1   teaspoon vanilla
⅔   cup fine dry bread crumbs
1   cup finely ground almonds (whirl nuts in blender or food processor)
1   cup (about ¼ lb.) grated milk chocolate
⅛   teaspoon cream of tartar
    Powdered sugar, or sweetened whipped cream and chocolate curls

Beat butter and ½ cup of the sugar together until creamy. Add egg yolks, one at a time, beating well after each addition. Beat in vanilla, bread

crumbs, almonds, and chocolate until blended.

In a separate bowl, beat egg whites and cream of tartar until soft peaks form. Gradually beat in remaining ½ cup sugar until mixture is stiff and glossy. Stir about a third of the beaten egg whites into butter mixture. Then, gently but thoroughly, fold in remaining egg whites. Spread batter in a well-greased, flour-dusted 9-inch spring-form pan.

Bake in preheated 325° convection oven for 40 to 50 minutes or until top is well browned and a wooden pick inserted in center comes out clean. Let stand in pan for 10 minutes; then remove sides and cool thoroughly. Before serving, dust with powdered sugar, or top with whipped cream and garnish with chocolate curls. Makes 8 to 10 servings.

SESAME POUND CAKE

The nutlike flavor of toasted sesame seeds gives this moist, rich cake a special touch. Look for sesame oil in stores where Chinese foods are sold.

⅓   cup sesame seeds
¾   cup butter or margarine, softened
1   cup sugar
1   teaspoon <u>each</u> vanilla, sesame oil, and grated lemon peel
4   eggs
2   cups all-purpose flour
½   teaspoon salt
1   teaspoon baking powder
½   cup milk

Spread sesame seeds in a shallow baking pan; bake in 325° convection oven for 15 to 20 minutes or until golden brown. Let stand until cool.

In large bowl of electric mixer

beat butter and sugar together until creamy. Beat in vanilla, oil, and lemon peel. Add eggs, one at a time, beating well after each addition.

In a separate bowl, combine flour, salt, and baking powder. Add all but 1 tablespoon of the sesame seeds. Add flour mixture to creamed mixture alternately with milk, stirring gently after each addition just until blended (do not overstir). Spread in a well-greased, flour-dusted 5 by 9-inch loaf pan. Sprinkle with reserved sesame seeds.

Bake in preheated 275° convection oven for 1¼ to 1½ hours or until a wooden pick inserted in center comes out clean. Remove from pan and place on a wire rack to cool. Makes 8 to 10 servings.

FLUFFY LEMON CHEESECAKE

Made with cottage cheese and yogurt, this luscious cheesecake is light textured and low in calories.

- 1 package (6 oz.) zwieback, finely crushed
- ⅓ cup each melted butter or margarine and firmly packed brown sugar
- 1 pint (2 cups) small curd cottage cheese
- ¼ cup mild honey
- 4 eggs, separated
- ¼ teaspoon salt
- 1 teaspoon grated lemon peel
- 2 tablespoons lemon juice
- 1 teaspoon vanilla
- ½ pint (1 cup) unflavored yogurt
- ½ cup granulated sugar

Combine crushed zwieback, butter, and brown sugar and mix until crumbly; reserve ¾ cup. Press remaining crumbs evenly and firmly over bottom of a greased 9-inch spring-form pan. Bake in preheated 350° convection oven for 5 minutes; let cool.

In blender or food processor, combine cottage cheese, honey, egg yolks, salt, lemon peel, lemon juice, vanilla, and yogurt; blend or process until smooth. Beat egg whites until soft peaks form; gradually add granulated sugar, beating until stiff. Fold in cheese mixture until blended. Turn into prepared pan and sprinkle top with reserved crumbs.

Bake in preheated 250° convection oven for 1¼ hours or until cake jiggles only slightly when gently shaken. Turn off heat; leave cake in oven for 1 more hour. Cool thoroughly, then refrigerate. Makes 8 to 10 servings.

BLACK BOTTOM CUPCAKES

These delicious cupcakes have a sweet treasure of chocolate chips in their centers.

    Chocolate chip filling (recipe follows)
- 1½ cups all-purpose flour
- 1 cup sugar
- ¼ cup cocoa
- 1 teaspoon baking soda
- ½ teaspoon salt
- 1 cup water
- 5 tablespoons salad oil
- 1 tablespoon cider vinegar
- 1 teaspoon vanilla
    About ⅓ cup finely chopped walnuts

Prepare chocolate chip filling and set aside.

In a large bowl, combine flour, sugar, cocoa, soda, and salt. In a separate bowl, beat together water, oil, vinegar, and vanilla; gradually add to flour mixture and stir until well blended.

Fill 18 paper-lined cupcake cups about half full of batter. Top each with 1 tablespoon of the chocolate chip filling and about ½ teaspoon walnuts.

Bake in preheated 300° convection oven for 25 to 30 minutes or until tops spring back when gently pressed. Makes 18 cupcakes.

Chocolate chip filling. Beat together 1 large package (8 oz.) softened **cream cheese**, 1 **egg**, and ⅓ cup **sugar** until smooth. Stir in 1 package (6 oz.) **semisweet chocolate baking chips**.

CRUNCHY WALNUT PIE

Cinnamon spices a walnut pie that may remind you of pecan pie but is not quite as sweet. For best results, bake it several hours or even a day ahead.

-    Pastry for a single crust 8-inch pie
- 3 eggs
- ½ cup firmly packed brown sugar
- 1 cup light corn syrup
- ¼ teaspoon salt
- 1 teaspoon each ground cinnamon and vanilla
- ¼ cup butter or margarine, melted
- 1 cup broken walnuts or walnut halves

Prepare your favorite pastry or use a mix; roll out on a lightly floured board, then fit into an 8-inch pie pan. Flute edge and set aside.

In a bowl, beat eggs and combine with brown sugar, corn syrup, salt, cinnamon, vanilla, and butter; mix until well blended. Stir in nuts. Pour mixture into prepared pastry shell.

Bake in preheated 350° convection oven for 35 to 40 min-

(Continued on page 88)

Here's a quartet of convection-baked goodies to serenade your sweet tooth. Clockwise from the top you see crunch-top rhubarb pudding (recipe on page 94); pear almond torte baked in a bundt pan (recipe on page 84); chocolate pinwheel cookies (recipe on page 90); and strawberry lemon cream torte (recipe on page 92).

utes or until filling jiggles only slightly when pie is gently shaken. Let cool on a wire rack for at least 2 hours before cutting. When thoroughly cool, cover with foil and keep at room temperature. Makes 6 servings.

PUMPKIN CHEESE PIE

Combining the best qualities of both cheesecake and spicy pumpkin pie, this dessert has a light texture and refreshing flavor. Make the filling in a blender or food processor.

1½ cups small curd cottage cheese
1 tablespoon orange juice concentrate
1½ cups canned pumpkin
3 eggs
¾ cup sugar
1 teaspoon ground cinnamon
½ teaspoon each ground ginger and allspice
¼ teaspoon ground cloves
Pastry for a single crust 9-inch pie
Sweetened whipped cream (optional)

In a blender or food processor, combine cottage cheese and orange juice concentrate; blend or process until smooth. Add pumpkin, eggs, sugar, cinnamon, ginger, allspice, and cloves; blend or process until well combined.

Prepare your favorite pastry or use a mix; roll out on a lightly floured board, then fit into a 9-inch pie pan. Flute edge. Turn pumpkin mixture into pastry shell.

Bake in preheated 350° convection oven 1 to 1¼ hours or until a knife inserted in center comes out clean. Let stand until cool, then serve at room temperature, or refrigerate several

hours before serving. Garnish with sweetened whipped cream, if desired. Makes 6 to 8 servings.

SHREDDED APPLE CUSTARD PIE

Lighter than the classic apple pie but not as rich as a traditional custard pie, this combination owes its difference to shredded tart apples. Serve it warm or cool, plain or topped with whipped cream.

Pastry for a single crust 9-inch pie
4 eggs
¾ cup sugar
¼ cup butter or margarine, melted
1 teaspoon vanilla
½ teaspoon grated lemon peel
¼ teaspoon each ground cinnamon and nutmeg
About 3 large tart apples
Sweetened whipped cream (optional)

Prepare your favorite pastry or use a mix; roll out on a lightly floured board, then fit into a 9-inch pie pan. Flute edge and set aside.

Lightly beat eggs; add sugar and beat until well blended.

Stir in butter, vanilla, lemon peel, cinnamon, and nutmeg.

Peel apples and coarsely shred with a food processor or a shredder with large holes; you should have 3 cups, lightly packed. Stir apples into egg mixture; spread filling in pastry shell.

Bake in preheated 350° convection oven for 45 to 50 minutes or until a knife inserted in center comes out clean. Let stand on a wire rack to cool. Serve warm or chilled. Garnish with dollops of sweetened whipped cream, if desired. Makes 6 to 8 servings.

YOGURT CHEESE PIE

Serve a topping of raspberries or sliced nectarines or peaches to brighten wedges of this cheesecake-like pie.

1¾ cups graham cracker crumbs
¾ cup sugar
⅓ cup butter or margarine, melted
1 large package (8 oz.) cream cheese, softened
3 eggs
2 teaspoons vanilla
¼ teaspoon salt
1 pint (2 cups) unflavored yogurt
2 cups raspberries or sliced nectarines, sweetened to taste

Combine crumbs, ¼ cup of the sugar, and butter. Press mixture evenly and firmly over bottom and sides of a 10-inch pie pan. Bake in 350° convection oven for 5 minutes; let stand while preparing filling.

In large bowl of electric mixer, beat together cream cheese and remaining ½ cup sugar. Beat in eggs, one at a time; then beat in vanilla and salt and continue beating until mixture is light and creamy. Blend yogurt into mixture and pour mixture into crumb crust.

Bake in preheated 350° convection oven for 30 to 35 minutes or until dry when lightly touched. Cool, then refrigerate for at least 4 hours or until next day. To serve, cut in wedges and spoon sweetened fruit with its juices over each serving. Makes 8 servings.

RHUBARB APPLE BERRY PIE

Chunks of rhubarb mingle with sliced apples and strawberry jam in this sweet-tart pie. You can adjust the amount of sugar in the pie to suit the apple you choose. Use less sugar for golden delicious; more for tarter apples.

1½   pounds rhubarb, cut in ½-inch pieces (about 4 cups)
2½   cups thinly sliced, peeled apples
 ½   cup strawberry jam
 ½   to ¾ cup sugar
3½   tablespoons quick-cooking tapioca
     Pastry for a double crust 9-inch pie
2   tablespoons butter or margarine

Stir together rhubarb, apples, jam (crush large pieces), sugar, and tapioca until blended; set aside.

Prepare your favorite pastry or use a mix. Divide pastry in half. On a lightly floured board, roll out each half into a 12-inch circle. Ease one circle into a 9-inch pie pan; spread filling in crust and dot with butter. Place other pastry circle over filling; trim and flute edge. Make several slashes in top of pie crust.

Bake in preheated 350° convection oven for 45 to 55 minutes or until crust is browned and fruit is tender. Makes 6 to 8 servings.

LEMON CAKE PIE

As this single crust pie bakes, a cakelike topping forms over the tart-sweet lemon filling.

     Pastry for single crust 9-inch pie
1½   cups sugar
2   tablespoons butter or margarine, melted
 ⅓   cup all-purpose flour
 ¼   teaspoon salt
 ½   teaspoon grated lemon peel
5   tablespoons lemon juice
3   eggs, separated
1¼   cups milk

Prepare your favorite pastry or use a mix; roll out on a lightly floured board, then fit into a 9-inch pie pan. Flute edge and set aside.

Stir together sugar and melted butter; blend in flour, salt, lemon peel, and lemon juice. Beat egg yolks, combine with milk, and stir into lemon mixture. In a large bowl, beat egg whites until stiff, moist peaks form; fold gently into lemon mixture, then pour into pastry shell.

Bake in preheated 350° convection oven for 45 to 55 minutes or until top is richly browned and set when lightly touched. Let stand on a wire rack to cool. Serve at room temperature, or refrigerate for as long as 6 hours. Makes 6 to 8 servings.

MERINGUE COOKIES

Dates and nuts add flavor and crunch to these puffy cookies. What a delicious way to use up leftover egg whites.

2   egg whites
     Dash of salt
1   cup each sugar, chopped walnuts, and chopped dates
1   teaspoon vanilla

In the top of a double boiler, beat egg whites until stiff, moist peaks form. Add salt and gradually beat in sugar. Place over boiling water and continue beating until mixture is sugary around edge. Add walnuts, dates, and vanilla; mix well. Drop batter by rounded teaspoons onto well-greased baking sheets.

Bake in preheated 250° convection oven for about 1 hour or until cookies are set and firm. Remove carefully from baking sheets and let stand on wire racks to cool. Store tightly covered. Makes 3 dozen cookies.

WALNUT CHEWS

Nuts—lots of them—replace most of the flour in these chewy drops, made without any butter or shortening.

1   cup firmly packed brown sugar
1   tablespoon flour
1   egg white
 ⅛   teaspoon cream of tartar
 ¾   teaspoon vanilla
1¼   cups finely chopped walnuts

In a bowl, mix sugar and flour. In another bowl, beat egg white and cream of tartar until moist, stiff peaks form; fold into sugar mixture until moistened. Lightly mix in vanilla and walnuts. Drop batter by rounded teaspoons onto greased, flour-dusted baking sheets.

Bake in preheated 275° convection oven for about 20 minutes or until set and lightly browned. Let stand on baking sheets for about 5 minutes; then cool on wire racks. Makes about 2½ dozen 2-inch cookies.

FROSTED APPLE COOKIES

Studded with apples and raisins, these spicy cookies travel well in lunchboxes or brown bags.

- ½ cup (¼ lb.) butter or margarine, softened
- 1⅓ cups firmly packed brown sugar
- 1 egg
- 2 cups all-purpose flour
- 1 teaspoon each baking soda and ground cinnamon
- ½ teaspoon each salt, ground cloves, and ground nutmeg
- ¼ cup apple juice or milk
- 1 cup each finely chopped, peeled apples and raisins
  Apple frosting (recipe follows)

Beat butter and sugar together until creamy; beat in egg. Sift flour with soda, cinnamon, salt, cloves, and nutmeg. Add flour mixture to creamed mixture alternately with apple juice. Fold in apples and raisins. Drop by level tablespoons onto well-greased baking sheets.

Bake in preheated 350° convection oven for 8 to 10 minutes or until golden brown. Remove from baking sheets. Prepare apple frosting and spread on cookies while they are still slightly warm. Makes about 4½ dozen cookies.

Apple frosting. Beat together 2 tablespoons softened **butter** or margarine and 1½ cups sifted **powdered sugar** until creamy. Beat in ¼ teaspoon **vanilla**, dash of **salt**, and about 2 tablespoons **apple juice** or milk to make a good consistency for spreading.

CRISP GINGER THINS

These tender, crisp little wafers are a delicious accent with fruit or puddings. Stored tightly covered, they keep well for as long as two weeks.

- ¾ cup butter or margarine, softened
- 1 cup sugar
- 1 egg
- ¼ cup molasses
- 2 cups all-purpose flour
- 2 teaspoons baking soda
- ½ teaspoon salt
- 1½ teaspoons ground ginger
- 1 teaspoon ground cinnamon
  Sugar

Beat butter and the 1 cup sugar together until creamy. Beat in egg and molasses. Combine flour, soda, salt, ginger, and cinnamon and add to creamed

mixture, stirring until thoroughly blended. Cover dough and refrigerate for at least 2 hours or until next day.

Sprinkle sugar on a piece of wax paper. Pinch off a piece of dough, roll into a 1-inch ball, and roll in sugar to coat. Repeat with remaining dough. Place balls about 2 inches apart on ungreased baking sheets.

Bake in preheated 300° convection oven for 10 to 12 minutes or until tops are almost firm. Let stand on baking sheets for about 3 minutes; then transfer to wire racks to cool. Makes about 6 dozen 2-inch cookies.

CHOCOLATE PINWHEEL COOKIES

Pictured on page 87

Two winning flavors, peanut butter and chocolate, are combined in these swirled refrigerator cookies.

- ½ cup (¼ lb.) butter or margarine, softened
- ½ cup smooth peanut butter
- ½ cup each granulated sugar and firmly packed brown sugar
- 1 egg
- 1¼ cups all-purpose flour
- ½ teaspoon each baking soda, salt, and ground cinnamon
- 1 package (6 oz.) semisweet chocolate baking chips

In a large bowl, beat butter, peanut butter, and both sugars until light and creamy. Add egg and beat well. Combine flour with soda, salt, and cinnamon; add to creamed mixture and blend well. Cover tightly and refrigerate for 2 hours or until firm.

Melt chocolate over hot water; cool slightly. On wax

paper pat chilled dough into a 12-inch square. Spread chocolate evenly over dough to within ½ inch of edges. Roll up tightly like a jelly roll; then cut in half. Wrap each roll well and refrigerate for several hours or until next day.

Remove 1 roll at a time; cut into ¼-inch-thick slices. Place slices ½ inch apart on ungreased baking sheets. Bake in preheated 325° convection oven for 8 to 10 minutes or until lightly browned. Let stand on baking sheets for a few minutes, then transfer to wire racks to cool. Makes about 4 dozen cookies.

ORANGE-WALNUT SHORTBREAD

Drizzle orange glaze over this shortbread, then cut it into morsels to serve for a special sweet treat.

1¼ cups all-purpose flour
¼ cup sugar
⅛ teaspoon salt
2 teaspoons grated orange peel
½ cup (¼ lb.) firm butter or margarine
1 cup finely chopped walnuts
1 tablespoon orange juice
Orange glaze (recipe follows)

In a bowl, combine flour, sugar, salt, and orange peel. With 2 knives or a pastry blender, cut in butter until mixture is very crumbly and no large particles remain. Mix in ¾ cup of the nuts and orange juice. With your hands, shape mixture into a firm ball and press evenly and firmly over bottom of a greased 7 by 11-inch baking pan.

Bake in preheated 275° convection oven for 40 to 45 minutes or until pale golden brown. Cool

slightly. Prepare orange glaze. Sprinkle shortbread with remaining ¼ cup nuts, and drizzle evenly with orange glaze. Cut into 1¼-inch squares, then let stand in pan to cool thoroughly. Makes 4 to 5 dozen cookies.

Orange glaze. Blend together 1 cup **powdered sugar,** ½ teaspoon **grated orange peel,** and 2 tablespoons **orange juice** until smooth.

APRICOT-COCONUT BARS

Moist and delicious, these powdered-sugar-dusted cookies have a piquant apricot flavor. Take them along in their baking pan for a family outing.

¾ cup all-purpose flour
¾ teaspoon baking powder
½ teaspoon salt
½ cup (¼ lb.) butter or margarine, softened
1 cup firmly packed brown sugar
2 eggs
¼ teaspoon almond extract
½ cup flaked coconut
1 cup finely chopped uncooked dried apricots
Powdered sugar

Mix flour, baking powder, and salt; set aside. In a large bowl, beat butter and sugar together until creamy; add eggs and almond extract and beat until fluffy. Gradually beat in flour mixture. Add coconut and apricots; mix until blended. Spread in a greased, flour-dusted 9-inch-square baking pan.

Bake in preheated 300° convection oven for 25 to 35 minutes or until top springs back when lightly pressed. Loosen edges with a spatula. Let stand in pan on a wire rack to cool completely; then cut into 1 by 2-inch bars. Sift powdered sugar over bars. Makes 32 cookies.

LEMON-NUT SQUARES

Made with granola and walnuts, these appealing bar cookies are delicious with ice cream or sherbet for dessert.

1 cup all-purpose flour
⅓ cup butter or margarine, softened
2 eggs
1 cup firmly packed brown sugar
¾ cup granola-type cereal
½ cup chopped walnuts
⅛ teaspoon baking powder
¾ teaspoon vanilla
1 teaspoon grated lemon peel
1½ tablespoons lemon juice
1 cup sifted powdered sugar

In a bowl, combine flour and butter and mix with your fingers until crumbly. Press evenly into bottom of a greased 8-inch-square baking pan. Bake in preheated 350° convection oven for 15 minutes.

In a bowl, beat eggs lightly; beat in brown sugar, cereal, walnuts, baking powder, and vanilla. Remove baking pan from convection oven and reduce oven temperature to 300°. Pour cereal mixture evenly over partially baked crust and return to convection oven. Bake for 20 to 25 minutes or until top is set and well browned. Let stand on a wire rack for 20 minutes.

In a bowl, beat lemon peel and lemon juice with powdered sugar until smooth. Spread over partially cooled cooky mixture. Cool thoroughly and cut into about 1½-inch squares. Makes 25 cookies.

CHEWY CHOCOLATE CHIP BARS

You sprinkle chocolate chips on top of the batter, but they don't stay there—they melt to form a yummy center layer.

Crust mixture (recipe follows)
1 egg
⅔ cup firmly packed brown sugar
1 teaspoon vanilla
2 tablespoons all-purpose flour
½ teaspoon baking powder
⅛ teaspoon salt
¾ cup finely chopped walnuts
½ cup semisweet chocolate baking chips

Prepare crust mixture. Pat evenly over bottom of a greased 8-inch-square baking pan. Bake in preheated 300° convection oven for 10 minutes. Let stand on a wire rack to cool.

In the same bowl in which crust mixture was prepared, beat egg. Add brown sugar and beat until blended. Mix in vanilla, flour, baking powder, salt, and walnuts. Spread evenly over crust. Sprinkle top with chocolate chips.

Bake in preheated 300° convection oven for 20 to 25 minutes or until golden brown. Let stand in pan on a wire rack until cool; then cut into 1⅓ by 2-inch bars. Makes 2 dozen cookies.

Crust mixture. In a small bowl, mix ⅓ cup softened **butter** or margarine with ⅓ cup firmly packed **brown sugar** until creamy. Mix in ⅔ cup **all-purpose flour** until blended.

STRAWBERRY LEMON CREAM TORTE

Pictured on page 87

In a convection oven, meringues bake to special light crispness, a quality never more appreciated than in this handsome dessert. Fresh strawberries accent the satiny lemon custard and whipped cream filling.

Baked 9-inch meringue shell (recipe follows)
3 egg yolks
1 whole egg
¾ cup sugar
¼ cup lemon juice
1½ teaspoons grated lemon peel
3 tablespoons butter or margarine
½ cup whipping cream
Whipped cream
Whole strawberries

Prepare meringue shell.

In the top of a double boiler, beat egg yolks and whole egg until combined; mix in sugar, lemon juice, and lemon peel. Add butter. Place over simmering water and cook, stirring, until mixture thickens. Remove lemon custard from heat and refrigerate until cool.

Whip cream until stiff; spread in bottom of cool meringue shell. Spread lemon custard over cream. Refrigerate for several hours or until next day. To serve, remove pan side from meringue; garnish top of torte with whipped cream and strawberries ar-

ranged decoratively in a ring. Makes 8 servings.

Meringue shell. In a bowl, beat 3 **egg whites** with ¼ teaspoon **each** **salt** and **cream of tartar** until soft peaks form. Gradually beat in ¾ cup **sugar**; then beat until stiff. Spread evenly in a greased, flour-dusted 9-inch spring-form pan, covering bottom and sides to about ½ inch below top edge. Bake in preheated 275° convection oven for 50 minutes to 1 hour or until firm and lightly browned. Let stand in convection oven with fan on and temperature at lowest setting (below 150°) for 1 hour.

CINNAMON-CHOCOLATE TORTE

Here is another spectacular meringue dessert—a cinnamon-spiced meringue shell containing whipped cream and a mousselike chocolate filling.

Cinnamon meringue shell (recipe follows)
1 package (6 oz.) semisweet chocolate baking chips
2 egg yolks
¼ cup water
½ pint (1 cup) whipping cream
¼ cup sugar
¼ teaspoon ground cinnamon
½ cup whipping cream (optional)
Chocolate curls or walnut halves (optional)

Prepare meringue shell.

Melt chocolate chips in the top of a double boiler over hot water. Spread 2 tablespoons of the hot chocolate over bottom of meringue shell; set aside. Add egg yolks and water to remaining warm chocolate and beat until smooth. Refrigerate mixture.

Combine the ½ pint cream with sugar and cinnamon and whip until stiff. Spread half the cream mixture over the chocolate-covered meringue shell. Fold remaining cream mixture into the chilled chocolate mixture and spread on top. Refrigerate for several hours or until next day. If desired, whip the ½ cup cream and use to garnish torte, along with chocolate curls or walnuts. Makes 8 servings.

Cinnamon meringue shell. In a bowl, beat 3 **egg whites** with ¼ teaspoon **salt** and ½ teaspoon **white vinegar** until soft peaks form. Mix ¼ teaspoon **ground cinnamon** into ½ cup **sugar** and gradually add to egg whites; beat until stiff and glossy. Place buttered wax paper on a greased baking sheet. Spread meringue on paper, forming a shell 8 inches across with sides 1¾ inches high and bottom ½ inch thick. Bake in preheated 275° convection oven for 1 to 1¼ hours or until meringue feels dry when lightly touched. Let stand in convection oven with fan on and temperature at lowest setting (below 150°) for 1 hour. Peel off paper.

NOCKERLN IN LEMON SAUCE

This elegant and sweet traditional dessert is called Salzburger Nockerln in Austria and Bavaria. Nockerln are airy egg dumpling puffs, a sort of sweet soufflé. This version bakes atop a refreshing lemon sauce and is served with strawberries.

As with any soufflé, this one must be served as soon as it is baked, but it goes together easily and bakes quickly. You can prepare the lemon sauce, separate the eggs, and measure the ingredients ahead of time.

Lemon sauce (recipe follows)
4 eggs
⅛ teaspoon each salt and cream of tartar
⅓ cup sugar
2 tablespoons flour
1 teaspoon grated lemon peel
Powdered sugar
Whole strawberries (optional)

Preheat convection oven to 350°. Prepare lemon sauce and set aside.

Separate eggs, placing whites in a large bowl and yolks in a smaller bowl. Beat whites with salt and cream of tartar until soft peaks form. Gradually beat in sugar; beat until mixture is very stiff and glossy; set aside. With same beaters, beat yolks until lemon colored. Add flour and lemon peel and continue beating until yolks thicken. Gently fold yolk mixture into beaten egg whites.

Pour prepared lemon sauce into an 8 by 10-inch oval baking pan or shallow 1½-quart pan; spoon egg mixture in 3 large mounds over sauce.

Bake in center of preheated 350° convection oven for 10 to 12 minutes or until puffed and lightly browned. Remove from oven, dust with powdered sugar, and serve immediately, spooning lemon sauce over each serving. Garnish with strawberries, if desired. Makes 4 to 6 servings.

Lemon sauce. In a small pan over medium heat, melt 4 tablespoons **butter** or margarine. Combine ½ cup **sugar** and 2 teaspoons **cornstarch**; stir into butter. Add ½ teaspoon grated **lemon peel.** Remove from heat and gradually add ¼ cup **lemon juice.** Return to heat and cook, stirring, until sauce boils and becomes syrupy.

HOT CHOCOLATE PUFFS

Profiteroles au chocolat, a favorite French dessert, translates into tiny cream puffs filled with ice cream and topped with dark chocolate sauce.

½ cup water
¼ cup butter or margarine
¼ teaspoon salt
1 tablespoon sugar
½ cup all-purpose flour
2 eggs
Hot chocolate sauce (recipe follows)
16 small scoops vanilla or coffee ice cream

In a 2-quart pan, combine water, butter, salt, and sugar. Bring to a full rolling boil. Add flour all at once; remove from heat. With a wooden spoon, beat mixture vigorously until it is smooth and pulls away from sides of pan. Beat in eggs, one at a time, until mixture is smooth and glossy. Let mixture stand for 15 minutes.

Drop dough by tablespoonfuls 1½ inches apart onto greased baking sheets to make 16 puffs. Bake in preheated 325° convection oven for 25 to 30 minutes or until puffs are firm and golden brown. Cut a 2-inch slit in base of each puff. Let stand on wire racks to cool.

Prepare hot chocolate sauce.

To serve, split puffs crosswise and fill each with a scoop of ice cream. Place 4 puffs in each of 4 shallow serving dishes. Pour hot chocolate sauce over puffs. Makes 4 servings.

Hot chocolate sauce. Coarsely chop 6 ounces **semisweet chocolate.** Place in a heavy pan with ½ cup **whipping cream.** Over medium heat, stir until chocolate melts and blends smoothly with cream. Remove from heat; gradually stir in

2 tablespoons **brandy.** Makes about 1¼ cups sauce.

HONEY PEACH COBBLER

A drop biscuit topping made with whole wheat flour and honey covers this baked peach dessert. It is especially good served warm with vanilla ice cream.

1½   **pounds peaches, peeled, pitted, and sliced, <u>or</u> 1 package (1 lb.) unsweetened frozen peach slices, partially defrosted**

1½   **tablespoons lemon juice**

¼   **cup honey**

1   **tablespoon cornstarch, mixed with 1 tablespoon water**

1   **tablespoon butter or margarine**

   Whole wheat and honey topping (recipe follows)

   Vanilla ice cream (optional)

Place peaches in a shallow 1½-quart baking pan. Stir in lemon juice, honey, and cornstarch mixture. Dot with butter. Prepare topping and drop by spoonfuls onto fruit mixture.

Bake, uncovered, in a preheated 325° convection oven for 25 to 30 minutes or until well browned. Serve warm or cool, with ice cream if desired. Makes 4 servings.

Whole wheat and honey topping. In a bowl, stir together ⅔ cup **whole wheat flour,** 1 teaspoon **baking powder,** ¼ teaspoon <u>each</u> **salt** and **ground cinnamon,** and ⅛ teaspoon **ground nutmeg.** With 2 knives or a pastry blender, cut in 3 tablespoons firm **butter** or margarine until well blended. Combine ⅓ cup **milk** and 2 tablespoons

honey; stir into flour mixture just until blended.

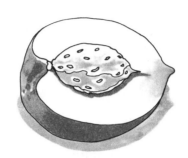

CRUNCH-TOP RHUBARB PUDDING

Pictured on page 87

The variable baking temperature for this rosy rhubarb dessert makes it a good choice to bake along with a roast.

6   **cups sliced rhubarb (about ¼-inch-thick slices)**

1   **cup granulated sugar**

2   **tablespoons cornstarch**

½   **cup water**

1   **teaspoon vanilla**

¾   **cup <u>each</u> all-purpose flour and firmly packed brown sugar**

½   **cup rolled oats**

1   **teaspoon ground cinnamon**

⅓   **cup butter or margarine, melted**

   Powdered sugar

   Whipped cream or vanilla ice cream (optional)

Place rhubarb in a 2-quart round or oval baking pan or 9-inch-square baking pan. In a pan, blend together granulated sugar and cornstarch. Stir in water. Over medium heat, bring mixture to a boil. Cook, stirring, until sauce becomes syrupy and clear; add vanilla. Pour liquid over rhubarb.

Mix together flour, brown sugar, oats, and cinnamon. Add

melted butter and mix until crumbly. Sprinkle topping evenly over rhubarb.

Bake, uncovered, in 300° to 350° convection oven for 45 minutes to 1 hour or until pudding is bubbly and top is browned.

Sprinkle with powdered sugar and serve warm or at room temperature with whipped cream (sweetened to taste) or vanilla ice cream, if desired. Makes 6 servings.

PEAR CRISP WITH CHEESE

The sharpness of Cheddar cheese enlivens this dessert made with winter pears.

4   **to 5 Anjou or bosc pears, peeled, cored, and sliced to make about 6 cups**

2   **tablespoons lemon juice**

½   **cup <u>each</u> all-purpose flour and sugar**

¼   **teaspoon <u>each</u> salt and ground cinnamon**

⅛   **teaspoon ground nutmeg**

¼   **cup butter or margarine**

⅔   **cup shredded sharp Cheddar cheese**

   Whipped cream or vanilla ice cream (optional)

Place pear slices in a greased 8 or 9-inch-square baking pan; drizzle with lemon juice. Combine flour, sugar, salt, cinnamon, and nutmeg. With 2 knives or a pastry blender, cut in butter until mixture is crumbly. Mix in cheese; sprinkle topping evenly over pears.

Bake, uncovered, in 300 to 350° convection oven for 45 minutes to 1 hour or until pears are bubbly and tender and topping is lightly browned. Serve warm or cool, with whipped cream (sweetened to taste) or ice cream, if desired. Makes 4 to 6 servings.

INDEX

METRIC CONVERSION TABLE

To change	To	Multiply by
ounces (oz.)	grams (g)	28
pounds (lbs.)	kilograms (kg)	0.45
teaspoons	milliliters (ml)	5
tablespoons	milliliters (ml)	15
fluid ounces (oz.)	milliliters (ml)	30
cups	liters (l)	0.24
pints (pt.)	liters (l)	0.47
quarts (qt.)	liters (l)	0.95
gallons (gal.)	liters (l)	3.8
Fahrenheit temperature (°F)	Celsius temperature (°C)	5/9 after subtracting 32